FITTER
Healthier
HAPPIER!

AN IMPORTANT NOTE
IT'S IMPORTANT TO REMEMBER THAT THIS
BOOK IS BASED ON WHAT HAS BEEN HELPFUL TO ME.
I'M NOT A TRAINED MEDICAL PROFESSIONAL, SO THE
CONTENT HERE ISN'T MEANT TO GIVE YOU A DIAGNOSIS,
CURE, OR PREVENT ANY ILLNESS. LAWS AND REGULATIONS
CHANGE OFTEN, SO IT'S IMPORTANT YOU SEEK OUT
UP-TO-DATE PROFESSIONAL ADVICE. REMEMBER, IF YOU
HAVE ANY QUESTIONS ABOUT YOUR PHYSICAL AND
MENTAL HEALTH, PLEASE SPEAK TO YOUR
DOCTOR OR A TRUSTED ADULT.

First published in the United Kingdom by HarperCollins *Children's Books* in 2024
HarperCollins *Children's Books* is a division of HarperCollins*Publishers* Ltd
1 London Bridge Street
London SE1 9GF

www.harpercollins.co.uk

HarperCollins*Publishers*
Macken House, 39/40 Mayor Street Upper
Dublin 1, D01 C9W8, Ireland

2

Text copyright © Joe Wicks 2024
Illustrations copyright © Kate Sutton 2024
Additional images: Shutterstock

ISBN 978—0—00—850104—4

Printed and Bound in the UK using 100% Renewable Electricity
at CPI Group (UK) Ltd

MIX
Paper | Supporting
responsible forestry
FSC™ C007454

Find out more about HarperCollins and the environment at
www.harpercollins.co.uk/green

**This publisher and the author disclaim liability for any medical and/or legal outcomes that
may occur as a result of applying the methods described by the author in this book.**

JOE WICKS

FITTER Healthier HAPPIER!

Your guide to a healthy
body and mind

Written with
STEVE COLE

Illustrated by
KATE SUTTON

HC
CB

HARPERCOLLINS
CHILDREN'S BOOKS

To all my favourite little people in the world.
My hilarious children Indie, Marley and Leni.
My beautiful nephews Oscar and Milo.
And all the other cool kids: Gray, Goldie, Sid,
Henry, Polly, Maeve, Winter, Rocky, Neo and Rio.
– J.W.

CONTENTS

INTRODUCTION

I'm **Joe Wicks**, aka **The Body Coach**.
You might remember me from my
PE With Joe online workouts,
where I bounced around my living
room in fancy-dress costumes to
get you all moving.

I work as a fitness coach and
I'm here to inspire and
motivate you to fall in love with
exercise and healthy food. My goal
is to help people live healthier and
happier lives and I believe this comes
down to four very important
factors: **movement**,
nutrition, **sleep** and a
calm mind.

Ever since I was seven years old, I've been fascinated by the human body and specifically how movement and exercise have the power to change how we feel!

I had quite a challenging childhood and my house was often very chaotic and stressful. This meant I found it very hard to focus in school and was often easily distracted and disruptive in class. People called me naughty, but deep down I knew I wasn't. I just bottled up my emotions and didn't know how to ask for help.

I know now that the most important thing to do is speak up and get help.

IF YOU ARE STRUGGLING WITH YOUR EMOTIONS, IT CAN HELP TO SPEAK TO A TRUSTED ADULT. YOU CAN ALSO CHECK OUT **PAGE 191** FOR SOME CHARITIES AND NETWORKS THAT CAN HELP.

However, something amazing happened to me in primary school. A moment that changed my whole life. I discovered PE!

I discovered a great way to release all that energy from my body. I found something I was good at and – even better! – something I loved. My PE teachers didn't see me as a naughty kid who couldn't sit still. They saw a boy who had loads of energy that could be used in a positive way through sport and exercise. The PE teachers were my favourite!

They understood me and inspired me. It was like someone had switched on a lightbulb and I realised that by running, jumping, skipping, hopping, laughing and playing I could change the way I felt in my mind.

I could get rid of my fear, anger, anxiety and frustration. Pushing yourself physically and having a positive attitude towards exercise and hard work can really help you in all areas of your life.

This is the reason I'm so passionate about writing this book and working with people just like you! I want to help you learn about and understand your body. If you can start to love exercise and healthy eating now, then you're far more likely to go on to live an active, healthy life.

Life will always throw challenges at you and there will be ups and downs, but this book will help you develop the tools you need to get through those stressful and difficult times. Our modern lives are very busy and filled with technology and social media – so it's more important than ever to prioritise exercise, nutrition and sleep to make sure we have a calm mind.

In chapter 1, **Know Your Body**, we discover what a healthy body looks like and how to get one! We'll explore the human body and discover how exercise affects our heart, lungs, muscles, our brain and so much more.

Then in chapter 2, **Fuel Your Body**, we'll look at nutrition and the importance of food for energy, muscles, joints, gut health and also our mental health. We will find out how different foods affect our bodies and I'll share some of my favourite foods with you!

In chapter 3, **Move Your Body** we'll look at getting our bodies moving and the way exercise improves our health, concentration and happiness. I'll also share top tips for improving fitness and strength with some workouts you can follow.

In chapter 4, **Focus Your Body**, we look at sleep! It's essential for our mental health and I'll give you my advice on getting a good night's rest. Without sleep, everything else falls apart, so if we can get this right we'll be winning!

Finally, we will learn about the small steps we can take to keep a **calm mind** in a busy, modern world. We'll investigate how too much screen time and social media affects our mind and learn ways to reduce stress and anxiety and improve our confidence and how we feel about ourselves.

Now the first thing to remember is that these factors are all linked – you can't have one without the other. That's why I call this . . .

. . . THE CIRCLE OF HAPPINESS.

CALM MIND → SLEEP

NUTRITION ← MOVEMENT

They are each as important as the other
for building a healthy and happy body.

I hope you enjoy reading this book as much as I've enjoyed writing it, and remember that small changes make a big difference.

So, what are you waiting for? Let's get started!

Happy reading!

Love Joe

CHAPTER 1

KNOW YOUR BODY!

Right! Everyone knows it's important to stay healthy. But how does eating well, exercise and good mental health actually help us – and what else does our body need?

LET'S FIND OUT!

Well, to answer those questions, let's take a deep dive into the magnificent human body. It is made up of over fifty chemical elements. The four key elements are . . .

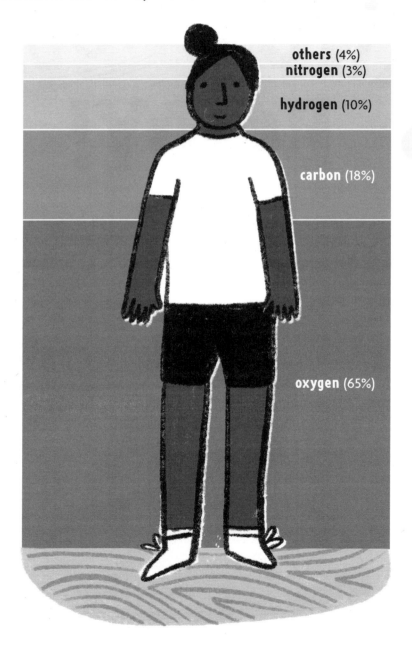

others (4%)
nitrogen (3%)
hydrogen (10%)
carbon (18%)
oxygen (65%)

These chemical elements join together to make cells. In the average human body, there are around **37 trillion** cells. There are over 200 different types of cell and they come in all shapes and sizes. Cells of a similar type work together to create body tissue. Some of this body tissue is then joined to form our organs.

Your body is like a machine. It's made up of lots of systems that are in charge of everything from growing the hair on your head to letting you know when you need a wee. These bodily systems literally keep you alive, so let's take a closer look at them.

CAN ANYONE GUESS WHERE WE'RE GOING TO START? WE'LL BEGIN WITH THE HARDEST OF THEM ALL . . .

THE SKELETON

We can't see our skeleton because it's hidden under our skin – well, except at Halloween when you might spot a few walking about by themselves!

In humans, the skeleton gives your body its shape and form. It's like a framework made of bones (which are extremely hard) and connective tissue, such as cartilage, tendons and ligaments (which are far more flexible than our bones). Muscles and connective tissues form round our bones.

GUESS WHAT?

There are 206 bones in the average body and they make up about 15% of our body weight!

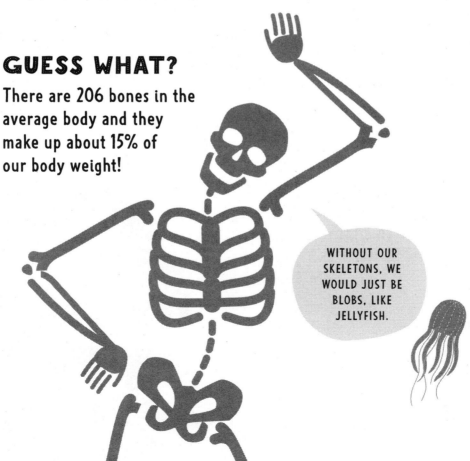

WITHOUT OUR SKELETONS, WE WOULD JUST BE BLOBS, LIKE JELLYFISH.

OUR SKELETON IS THERE TO HELP WITH THREE IMPORTANT THINGS:

MOVEMENT – it helps you to run, sit, walk, jump and lots more!

PROTECTION – it protects your inner organs.

SUPPORT – it holds your body upright.

21

Bones

Bones are built to be both hard AND flexible. This means they're less likely to break if they get knocked or bumped.

The outer layer of a bone is very hard, but inside it has a spongy layer that is like honeycomb – so it has lots of tiny spaces in it. This makes a bone very light but strong too. It also contains stretchy **collagen** – which keeps a bone flexible. In the centre of certain bones you will find bone marrow, which has a very important function – to produce red and white blood cells and platelets. We'll discuss this in more detail later!

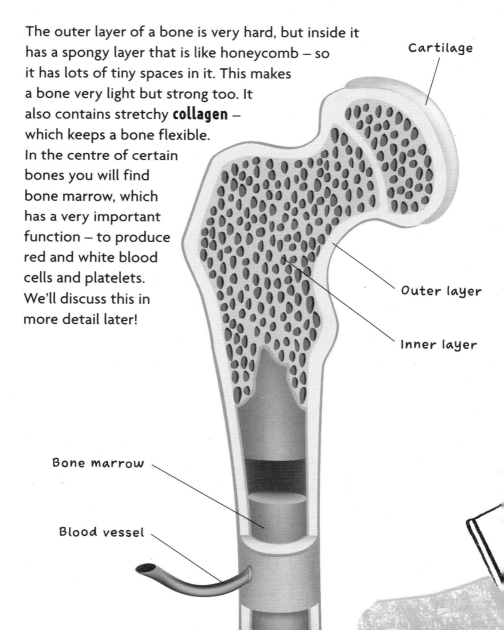

Cartilage

Outer layer

Inner layer

Bone marrow

Blood vessel

The skeleton is strong, but luckily it's also very light — having a heavy skeleton would make it very difficult to move about. Exercise is very important for healthy bones. Running, jumping, climbing and walking are all weight-bearing activities — the weight of your muscles and the weight of gravity both put pressure on your bones. When bones bear pressure regularly, they grow stronger.

WHICH MEANS YOU GET STRONGER TOO!

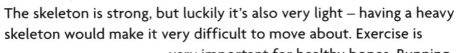

SKELETON FACTS:
Longest, strongest, heaviest bone: your thigh bone or femur.
Shortest bone: your stirrup, which is found in your ear. You couldn't hear without it!

Joints

Where two or more bones meet in the skeleton, you will find a joint. Some joints aren't flexible – like the joints which are found linking the bones in your skull. They are pretty solid! Other joints let you have just a bit of movement – like the discs in your spine, which allow you to bend your back. But most joints can move around easily.

There are many different types of free-moving joints in the body, and they each allow parts of our body to move in different ways. These joints are filled with a special fluid that stops any nasty rubbing or damage between the bones. Let's talk about three joints in particular.

Raise your right arm in the air. Put your left hand on your right shoulder. Now draw big circles in the air with your right arm. Can you feel the way the arm moves? This is an example of a **ball-and-socket joint**.

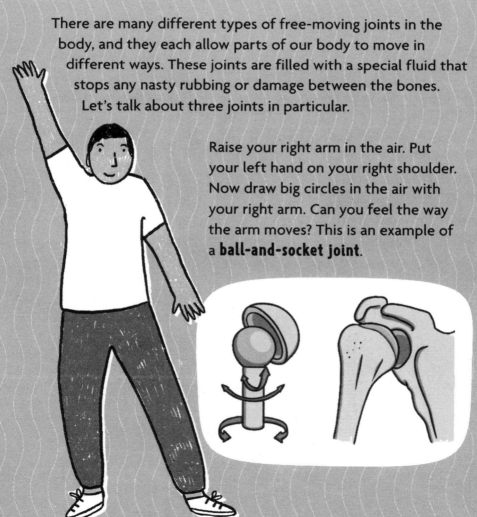

If you bend your elbow or your knee, you're using a **hinge joint**. Like the name suggests, one bone moves while the other stays still, like the hinge on a door.

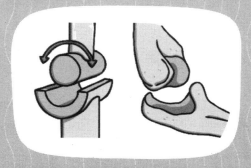

Wave your hand — you're using a **plane joint**. If you waggle your foot from side to side, you're using another! Plane joints allow a gliding movement.

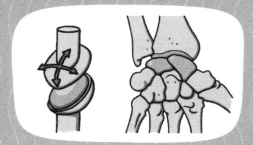

We shouldn't forget **ligaments** either! They often connect two bones together, particularly in the joints. They work like clever ropes, holding the ends of two bones together so they can't twist too far or become dislocated.

EXERCISE IS VERY IMPORTANT FOR YOUR JOINTS AS IT WILL STOP THEM GETTING STIFF. YOU SHOULD ALWAYS WARM UP AND COOL DOWN BEFORE YOU EXERCISE – WHICH WE'LL COVER IN CHAPTER 3.

CHALLENGE: Single-leg Box Step-up

1. Stand at the bottom of some stairs. Place one hand on the banister rail.

2. Step with your left foot on to the first stair.

3. Now drive your right leg upwards into the air.

4. Hold it there for a second, then place your right foot back down on the ground.

5. Repeat with the left leg.

Try doing ten of these in a row, each day, for a week!

| DAY 1 | DAY 2 | DAY 3 | DAY 4 | DAY 5 | DAY 6 | DAY 7 |

Don't worry if you are a bit wobblier on one leg than the other (most people are!) – but keep practising. If you can do these exercises every day for seven days, by the end of the week, you should feel much stronger.

JOE KNOWS

A bit of aching after exercise is healthy – it shows your muscles are working and getting stronger. But if any exercise starts to really hurt, stop. Check with an adult that you're doing it correctly.

27

MUSCLES

Muscles are amazing. They are made of soft tissue bunched together in long, stretchy fibres — and they literally hold us together. Without muscles, you wouldn't be able to move at all and your skeleton would fall apart. Some muscles you can choose to move with your brain. Some muscles work all by themselves.

That's one more reason why exercise is so important: it strengthens the muscles round the joints so that they stay strong and flexible. The more we use our muscles, the stronger they get! Whether you're running in a race, lifting something heavy or playing tag in the playground, those muscles will be helping you along — so it makes sense to look after them.

GUESS WHAT?

The word 'muscle' comes from a Latin word for 'mouse'. That's because early doctors thought that rippling muscles looked like mice running under the skin.

There are over 600 muscles in your body, so I can't list them all here. But let's look at some of the most important ones we use when we exercise.

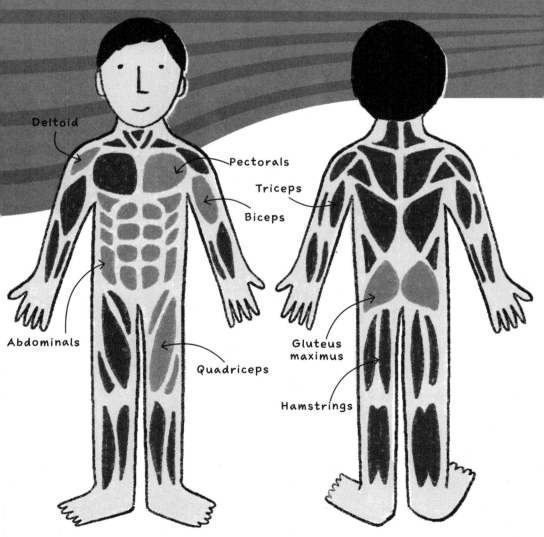

Deltoid

Pectorals

Triceps

Biceps

Abdominals

Quadriceps

Gluteus maximus

Hamstrings

CHALLENGE: Lunges

The lunge is a great workout for the muscles at the tops of your legs – your quadriceps and gluteus maximus!

1. Take a big step forward on one leg.
2. Lower your hips until both knees are bent. Don't let your front knee come over your toes.
3. Push back to your starting position.

For a start, try five of those on each leg. Want a harder challenge? See if you can do twenty lunges – ten on each leg – every day for a whole week!

Mega Muscles

There are many different types of muscle inside the human body. Let's explore them in a little more detail . . .

Skeletal muscles

These muscles tighten to move your bones. They can be found in your legs and arms. They are **voluntary** muscles, which means you can control what they do most of the time.

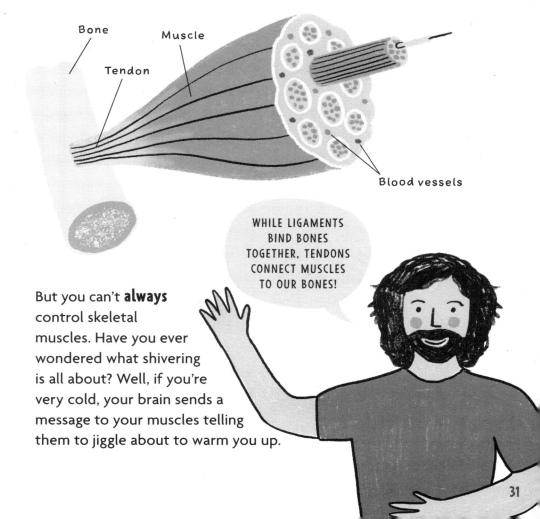

Bone

Muscle

Tendon

Blood vessels

WHILE LIGAMENTS BIND BONES TOGETHER, TENDONS CONNECT MUSCLES TO OUR BONES!

But you can't **always** control skeletal muscles. Have you ever wondered what shivering is all about? Well, if you're very cold, your brain sends a message to your muscles telling them to jiggle about to warm you up.

Face muscles

Some very important skeletal muscles are the face muscles, but they aren't all attached to bones. A lot of them are attached to the skin on your face, to help us make different expressions. Exercising THESE muscles is a lot of fun because we can pull funny faces . . .

HAHA!

HAHA!

. . . AND MAKING OURSELVES LAUGH IS REALLY GOOD FOR OUR MENTAL HEALTH!

HAHA!

Smooth muscles

This type of muscle is made up of layers. They get things done all over your body by tightening up and then relaxing. These muscles are **involuntary** muscles – you can't control them – they work without you even thinking about them every time you eat, or use your eyes to focus on something.

When relaxed, smooth muscles hold in your wee; when they tighten, it pushes the wee out.

Cardiac muscle

This muscle is found in the heart, and it keeps you alive. The cardiac muscle tightens to pump blood through the body, then relaxes to let it back into the heart again.

BUT BEFORE WE GET ON TO THE HEART, LET'S HEAD BACK TO . . . WELL, THE HEAD! BECAUSE BY STARTING THERE WE'LL FIND THE SYSTEM THAT ALLOWS ALL THESE MUSCLES TO ACT AND REACT.

THE BRAIN AND NERVOUS SYSTEM

Feeling nervous?

The nervous system is the command centre of the body – it carries messages from the brain to anywhere they need to go. The nervous system is made up of the brain, the spinal cord and trillions of nerves.

The human body is like an incredibly complex machine. Instead of wires running inside, connecting all the important bits to keep it working, it has **nerves**. Each nerve is a bundle of special cells called **neurons** that deliver electrical signals from your brain to different parts of your body, telling them what you want them to do. Many of these neurons travel along the **spinal cord** (imagine a very busy motorway in your body). It's a long, tube-like structure that runs from your brain to your lower back and is made up of nerves and cells that pass messages back and forth between the brain and the muscles.

GUESS WHAT?

Scientists say there are between 86 and 100 billion neurons in the average brain – and they send information shooting through your body at around 268 miles per hour!

For example, imagine you're out in the garden playing with a ball, and your friend throws it to you.

Your eyes see the ball coming towards you. Neurons pass this message along the nerve at the back of your eye to your brain.

Your brain then sends a message, along your nerves, to your arms and hands to get them to move, ready to catch the ball.

And all this happens in less than a second!

Without the neurons sending these electrical signals and sparking tiny chemical reactions inside you, you wouldn't be able to move your body, breathe, think or feel sensations like hot and cold.

The **sensory**, **motor** and **relay** neurons all work together to deliver messages around your body. For example, if you touch something sharp, your sensory neurons travel up to the brain, and pass the information on. Then your relay neurons form a link, and they pass this information to your motor neurons. The motor neuron controls the movement of the body, so it would cause you to move your hand away from the sharp object. Clever, eh?

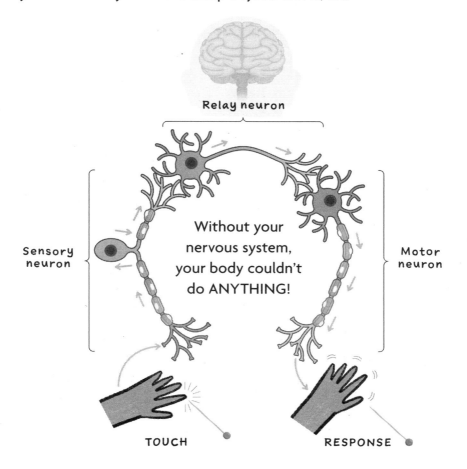

Relay neuron

Sensory neuron

Without your nervous system, your body couldn't do ANYTHING!

Motor neuron

TOUCH

RESPONSE

The Brain

The brain is the most complex organ in the body. It controls everything you do – including moving, thinking, feeling and your memory. It's like a supercomputer, but much more powerful. Think about all the different things you do each day – that's all thanks to your amazing brain.

The brain works all the time. Even while you're asleep and it reminds you to breathe . . . it even gives you dreams.

If we take a closer look at the brain, it appears like it is split into halves. These are called hemispheres and each one is divided into different sections. Each section has a special job to do.

THE FRONT AREA
This part of the brain deals with planning and solving problems. It's where your personality comes from.

THE SPEECH AND HEARING AREAS
These deal with sounds – they help us talk, listen and understand words.

THE LOWER SIDE LOBES
These parts of the brain handle our memories and emotions.

THE MOTOR AREA
This part of the brain controls how your muscles move.

THE SENSORY AREA
When we touch something, this helps us understand what it is we are feeling.

THE VISUAL AREA
This part of the brain turns the signals from our eyes into pictures that we can recognise.

THE CEREBELLUM
This allows the body to move smoothly – very helpful for exercise.

THE BRAINSTEM
This connects the brain and the spinal cord, which carries all the messages from your brain to your body and back again.

GUESS WHAT?

Your brain grows really fast when you're young. By the time you're one, it has tripled in size, and by the time you're twenty-five it will reach its full size.

The billions of neurons in the brain process your thoughts, tell you to move and control all the things that happen automatically in your body, such as breathing. It's no wonder that the brain uses around 20% of your energy supply. That's more than any other part of the body.

Don't think that we don't need to 'exercise' our brains because they're sitting inside our heads. Physical exercise is really important for our brain's health – for a start, it increases blood flow to the brain and releases **endorphins** – special chemicals produced in the brain that improve your mood!

Exercise helps us
to focus, learn and
stay happy!

The Ear

Your ears aren't only used for hearing. They help to balance you too. Each ear contains tiny tubes filled with liquid. When the liquid moves around, it tells your brain you're moving.

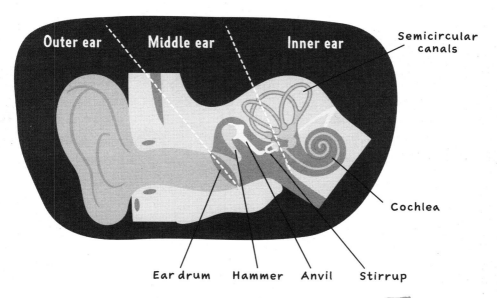

Outer ear | Middle ear | Inner ear | Semicircular canals

Ear drum | Hammer | Anvil | Stirrup

Cochlea

So, when you spin round and round, this makes the liquid swirl very quickly. In fact, it goes on swirling even when you've stopped.

THIS IS WHAT GIVES YOU THAT DIZZY FEELING.

CARDIOVASCULAR SYSTEM

The cardiovascular system is like a busy motorway that carries blood round our body. At the centre of it is the heart. The heart is the mighty engine of the body. It's roughly the size of a clenched fist, and it beats over 100,000 times each day!

The cardiovascular system is a loop and that's because the blood takes a special one-way route through the body. This is called **circulation**.

Blood

Blood is made up of plasma, a yellow liquid that carries three types of blood cell – **red blood cells**, **white blood cells** and **platelets**. They all have a different job to do:

Red blood cells carry oxygen round the body.

White blood cells are part of the immune system (our body's way of protecting us from harmful things) and help us fight illness.

Platelets help our blood to clot and stop us from bleeding inside and outside our body.

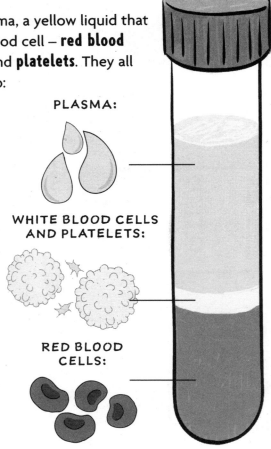

PLASMA:

WHITE BLOOD CELLS AND PLATELETS:

RED BLOOD CELLS:

Blood keeps us alive. Travelling through special pipes called **veins** and **arteries**, it carries oxygen and nutrients (substances found in food that are important for health and growth) to all parts of the body so they keep working. Blood helps remove the stuff the body doesn't want.

GUESS WHAT?

An average child has about 2.5 litres of blood inside them – that's roughly 8% of their body weight!

Ba-dum! Ba-dum!

Have you ever felt your heartbeat? It's the little valves that open and close inside the heart, pumping the blood round the body. These valves are like doors that open to let blood in and then quickly close again, to keep blood flowing in the right direction. And that *thump-thump*? That's the sound of the valves closing!

CHALLENGE: Rate Your Heart Rate

1. Gently place the first and middle finger of your right hand against the side of your neck, just under your jaw. You should be able to feel a little wave caused by your heart beating. This is called your **pulse**.

2. Now take a timer and set it for thirty seconds. Start the timer and count your pulse. Make a note of how many beats you count.

3. At the end of the thirty seconds, multiply the number you counted by two. Now you know how many times your heart beats in a minute when you're resting.

4. Next, do thirty seconds of star jumps.

5. Straight away, repeat the exercise. Has your heart rate changed? Is the number of beats per minute higher or lower? Can you guess?

30 SECONDS REPEAT

It takes less than one minute for blood to travel once round the body. If you do some very energetic exercise – like running, swimming or star jumps – you can sometimes feel your heart beating quite quickly. This just means it's working harder to push blood full of oxygen round your body to feed your muscles.

When you're exercising and your muscles *don't* get enough oxygen, you can get a cramp. This sudden tight pain is the muscles saying, **'Oi! Give me some oxygen!'** If you rest, the oxygen will top up and the feeling will soon pass.

The Heart

The journey starts when you breathe in air. The oxygen from the air is absorbed into your blood through thin blood vessels in the lungs.

The blood filled with oxygen leaves the lungs and travels into the left side of the heart. From here, it is pumped out to feed the rest of the body with oxygen.

As it does so, the blood starts to run out of oxygen and fill with waste gas — carbon dioxide. This is then carried to the right side of the heart. From here, it is pumped through to the lungs. You get rid of the carbon dioxide by breathing it out.

Then you take another breath. The oxygen is absorbed into your blood by blood vessels in the lungs . . .

. . . AND THE PROCESS STARTS ALL OVER AGAIN!

BREATHE OUT   BREATHE IN

6. Carbon dioxide leaves the body.

1. Oxygen enters the body.

2. The blood filled with oxygen leaves the lungs and travels into the left side of the heart.

LUNGS

5. Blood is carried to the right side of the heart to be pumped through to the lungs.

HEART

4. The blood runs out of oxygen and fills with waste gas.

3. Oxygen-rich blood circulates the body.

Now – take a deep breath! It's time to check out the . . .

49

RESPIRATORY SYSTEM

As you found out in the last section, your body needs a constant supply of oxygen to survive. And we get that from breathing. The respiratory system includes the nose, mouth, throat and lungs, and it allows your bloodstream to take oxygen to every cell in your body.

Nose knowledge

Our nose is there to help us breathe safely. Remember, it's not just air we pull into our lungs but all the particles that hang around in it – tiny specks like dirt, pollen, viruses and so on. That's why we have little hairs in our nose called **cilia** – they catch a lot of the small stuff so it can't harm us. Sometimes, if something irritating gets stuck up our nose, we get rid of it by **sneezing**.

GUESS WHAT?

A sneeze is very powerful – it can
send stuff shooting out of our nostrils
at over a hundred miles per hour!

Ever thought taste was just
something your tongue did?
Think again! Your nose plays an
important part too. The smell
from our food helps us to taste.
Take a bite of food and think
carefully about the taste. Then
hold your nose and take another
bite. Does it taste different?

The Mouth

We put food and drink into our body through our mouth. We can breathe through it too, but this isn't as good for us as breathing through our nose. For a start, we don't have little hairs in our mouth or down our throat to catch those pesky particles.

JOE KNOWS

Did you know we lose up to half a litre of water a day through breathing? You can see the tiny water droplets when you breathe on to a glass or a mirror. So it's important to drink plenty of water and stay hydrated.

The Throat

At the base of your throat are two tubes. The first tube is called the **oesophagus** and it takes food and drink to your stomach. The second tube is called your windpipe, or your **trachea** and it takes the air into your lungs.

Your windpipe also contains your vocal cords – you pass a stream of air over your vocal cords to form words and noises. You'd have no voice without them.

The Lungs

We have two lungs in our chest. They draw healthy oxygen into the body and push unhelpful carbon dioxide out. But our lungs are not built the same. The right lung is separated into three sections called **lobes**, while the left one only has two lobes. It's meant to be smaller – it's leaving some room for your heart!

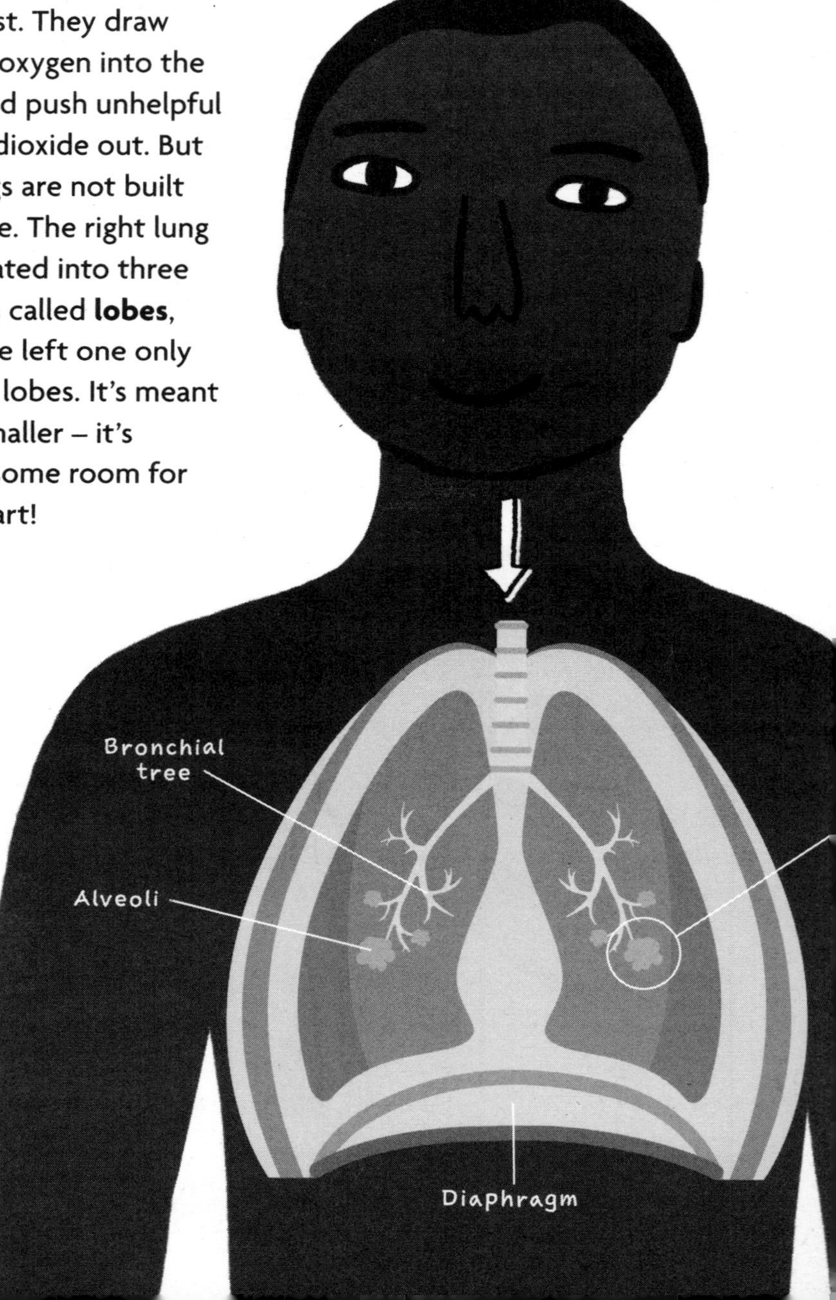

Bronchial tree

Alveoli

Diaphragm

Sitting at the bottom of the lungs is the **diaphragm**. This thin muscle helps us to breathe in and out. When the diaphragm relaxes, it moves up and squeezes your lungs to help push the air out. When it tenses it moves down to allow more air in.

Inside the lungs is a system of airways known as the **bronchial tree** – these carry air into your **alveoli**, little bags of air that allow your body to absorb oxygen and remove carbon dioxide.

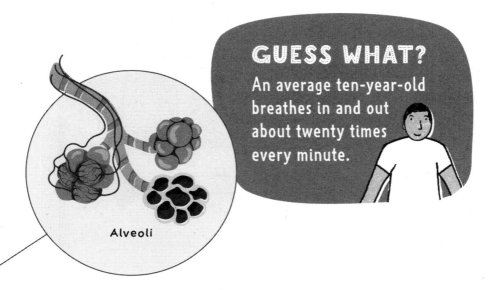

Alveoli

GUESS WHAT?
An average ten-year-old breathes in and out about twenty times every minute.

The more air your lungs can take in (your lung capacity), the more oxygen moves round your body – which means you can move and exercise better and faster.

Did you know you can increase your lung capacity by exercising regularly? This is especially handy if you're swimming since it's the air in our lungs that helps us float! If we breathe out in a swimming pool, our bodies have to work harder to stop us from sinking.

CHALLENGE: Make a Lung

If you want to see how we breathe in and out, you can make a working model of a lung in no time at all!

You will need:
A 500ml plastic water bottle
2 balloons
A craft knife
Scissors
An adult to help

I. Ask an adult to remove the bottom of the bottle with the craft knife.

2. Push the balloon inside the neck of the bottle. Don't let go – stretch the neck of the balloon over the bottle's neck.

3. With the scissors, cut off the top third of the second balloon. Tie a knot in this balloon's neck.

4. Stretch the open end of this balloon and place it securely over the wide opening at the bottom of the bottle.

5. Now gently pull back on the knot and then return it to its resting position. Watch what happens to the first balloon!

6. The knotted balloon is like the diaphragm. It tightens and air is pulled into the lungs. It relaxes and the air is pushed out!

PULL

THE DIGESTIVE SYSTEM

We power our bodies using the energy that we get from food. This is broken down by our digestive system and sorted into useful nutrients, which are absorbed into our blood. Anything that is left over is got rid of in our wee and poo.

It's really important that we put healthy food into our bodies. The right sorts of food don't only give us energy. They make our bodies strong, help us to grow and support our immune system to protect us from getting ill.

WHEN WE WANT FOOD BUT DON'T HAVE ANY, IT CAN SOMETIMES MAKE US ANGRY.

Eating helps our mind and mood. When we taste something delicious, it releases **endorphins** and makes us happy.

But what is it about food that gives us all these great things? Well, it's the **nutrients** – these are chemicals that can be found in food when it's broken down in our body. And what part of our body breaks it down? The **digestive system**, of course!

LET'S TAKE A CLOSER LOOK AT THE JOURNEY OUR FOOD TAKES AND HOW THESE NUTRIENTS GET INTO OUR BODIES.

A QUESTION OF DIGESTION

Before you even took the first bite of your breakfast today, your digestive system went to work and for hours afterwards it was busy breaking down all the food.

Within the **first ten seconds** of eating, you begin chewing your food into little bits and the **saliva** in your mouth helps to break it down before it moves into your stomach.

Four hours in and your food is being turned into a liquid.

After **seven hours**, your intestines are busy sorting out all the good nutrients and absorbing them into your blood.

And finally, between **24–72 hours** later, anything that isn't useful is turned into poo or wee and leaves your body.

Well, that's it in a nutshell . . . but digestion is far more complicated than that.

SO LET'S TAKE A LOOK AT EACH STAGE IN MORE DETAIL.

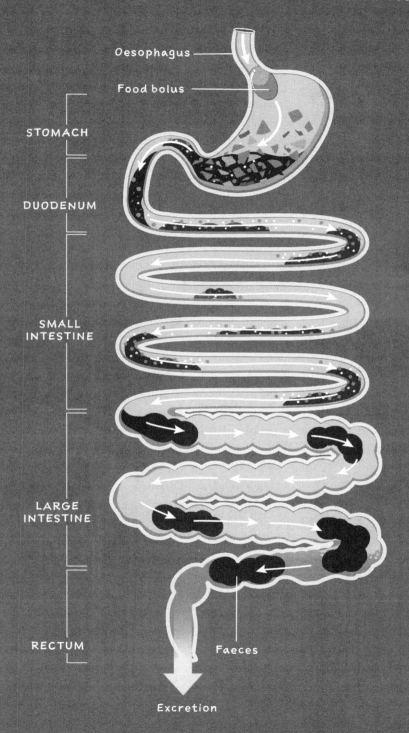

Oesophagus

Food bolus

STOMACH

DUODENUM

SMALL
INTESTINE

LARGE
INTESTINE

RECTUM

Faeces

Excretion

Saliva

Some foods have a mouthwatering smell or taste and that 'mouth water' is called **saliva**. As you chew your food and push it round your mouth with your tongue, saliva starts breaking it down – while the moisture makes the food stick together into something easier to swallow. As well as helping to break down food, saliva has many other benefits including protecting your tooth enamel from decay and stopping bad breath.

But where does the food go after the mouth?

HAVE YOU EVER NOTICED THAT IF YOU CHEW BREAD FOR A LONG TIME IT STARTS TO TASTE SWEET? THIS IS BECAUSE YOUR SALIVA BEGINS TO BREAK DOWN THE STARCH IN THE BREAD AND TURNS IT TO SUGAR!

Salivary glands

Epiglottis

Oesophagus

This is a stretchy pipe that lets food pass from the back of your throat to your stomach. It mustn't be muddled up with another pipe at the back of your throat – your windpipe (or trachea), which you use to breathe!

Because no one wants chewed-up food in their lungs, the human body comes with a helpful flap called the **epiglottis** that blocks the opening to your windpipe to make sure that food only goes down the oesophagus.

In a few seconds, the muscles in your oesophagus squeeze the food down into your stomach.

Your epiglottis works automatically, but sometimes things get past it, especially if you're talking or laughing while you're eating, or you're not paying attention. The cough reflex starts straight away and usually fixes the problem by clearing your windpipe.

JOE KNOWS!

Most of the time, food and drink go down the right way. But have you ever swallowed something and started coughing? If you have, chances are an adult told you that your food or drink went down the wrong way.

63

Stomach

At the far end of the oesophagus is the
stomach. And I like the stomach! Not
just because of the very important job it
does in digesting our food, but because it's
shaped like the letter J – J for Joe!

Once the food you've eaten
arrives in your stomach, it's
stored there. The juices
in the stomach work with
the strong muscle walls to
break it down into a lumpy
liquid called **chyme.** When it's
mushy enough, this chyme is pushed
on to the next stage of its journey through your body.

Small intestine

The small intestine is a long tube around **2–3 centimetres** wide
that's bundled up under your stomach – and a better name
for it would be the pretty big intestine! The length varies from
person to person but usually it's between **2–8 metres** long. In
the small intestine, the food is broken down even further – into
nutrients. It's given a helping hand by the vital extra juices sent
along by the **liver**, the **pancreas** and the **gallbladder**. Then the
nutrients pass through the walls of the small intestine and into
the blood, where they are taken to the liver.

Liver

The liver sends extra juice to the small intestine to help break down the food. This juice, called **bile**, comes from the gallbladder and helps your blood to absorb fats. Once the nutrient-rich blood is sent to the liver, this clever organ sorts out what good stuff should go where. It stores some nutrients and turns what the body doesn't need into more bile.

Gallbladder

The gallbladder is in the top right of your stomach and it is home to the bile that your liver produces.

Pancreas

The pancreas sits behind your stomach and is extremely important for digestion. It produces **enzymes** that break down sugars, fats and starches.

Meanwhile, back in the small intestine, anything that isn't absorbed into the blood moves into the large intestine.

JOE KNOWS!
The liver is the only organ in your body that can regenerate itself if it gets damaged!

Large intestine

In the large intestine, the body removes the last remaining nutrients and the rest of the water from your food – but where is the stuff that can't be used going to go? Well, as it passes through, more and more water is absorbed from it until all that's left is something more solid: poo! And that poo is cleared out of the body when you go to the toilet.

The rumbly, squelchy noises your tummy makes are caused by food moving from the stomach into the intestines. When you eat or drink, you take in small amounts of air. This, along with the gases caused by digesting your food, starts to build up in your body. So your body has to find a way to get rid of them and it does this by . . . yes, you guessed it . . . farting or burping!

GUESS WHAT?

If you stretched out the large intestine and measured it, you'd find it's only about 1.5 metres long. That's way shorter than the small intestine – so why the name? Well, it's because of the width of the large intestine, which is about 5-6 centimetres. Much larger!

1.5 m

Large intestine

Whilst your digestive system removes waste food and nutrients, waste water and harmful chemicals are removed from our body by our kidneys and bladder.

Kidneys

Most people have two kidneys — they are shaped like kidney beans and can be found one on either side of your spine, under your rib cage. They are responsible for keeping your blood clean. They filter your blood and remove any unwanted water and chemicals and turn them into **urine** (wee). The urine then leaves your kidneys and travels down tubes to your bladder.

JOE KNOWS
Your kidneys work really hard! In 24 hours, they filter around 200 litres of fluid. That's lots.

Bladder

Your bladder is hollow and shaped like a balloon. It contains strong muscles and its job is to hold your urine until it's time for you to go to the toilet. When you need a wee, your bladder opens and the urine travels down a tube called the **urethra**.

It's very important to drink lots of water to help your kidneys and bladder work well and flush out all the harmful chemicals.

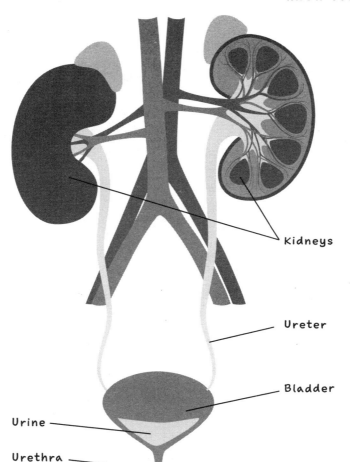

Kidneys

Ureter

Bladder

Urine

Urethra

WELL, WE'VE LEARNED
A LOT ABOUT THE HUMAN BODY.
AND THE BIG TAKEAWAY FROM ALL
THIS? BODIES ARE **INCREDIBLE!**
THE BEST WAY TO LOOK AFTER
YOURS IS TO EXERCISE
AND EAT WELL.

69

PROFESSOR JOE'S BODY QUIZ

Test how much you can remember from chapter 1 with this quick quiz! If you get stuck, flick back to the pages before.

1

Approximately, how many cells can be found in the average human body?

a) 37 b) 370 c) 37 million d) 37 trillion

2

Where are blood cells made?

a) Bone marrow b) Brain c) Lungs d) Tongue

3

What's your shortest bone called?

a) Saddle b) Stirrup c) Reins d) Bridle

4

Which organ controls everything in the nervous system?

a) Heart b) Liver c) Brain d) Skin

5

At what age does your brain reach its full size?

a) 1 b) 25 c) 40 d) 99

6

What element travels round your body in your red blood cells?

a) Oxygen b) Food
c) Neurons d) Saliva

7

What are the little hairs that line our nose called?

a) Plasma b) Cells c) Cilia
d) Alveoli

8

Why is your left lung smaller than your right lung?

a) To make room for your heart
b) Because it's younger
c) It's shrunk d) It doesn't do anything

9

Which organ produces enzymes to break down sugar and fats?

a) Heart b) Pancreas
c) Lungs d) Liver

10

On average, how long does it take food to travel through your digestive system?

a) 1 hour b) 30 minutes
c) 12 hours d) 24–72 hours

To check your answers turn to page 192.

CHAPTER 2

FUEL YOUR BODY!

Think of your body as a high-performance sports car. It runs best on good-quality fuel.

The fuel your body needs is food. Food gives us the energy to do everything from playing to walking to sleeping to thinking. So it makes sense that the better the food that you put into your body, the better it's going to work. If we only eat foods that aren't very good for us, then we won't operate as well – and we'll end up feeling tired and having no energy.

The Sensational Seven

There are seven **essential nutrients** that the body needs. Your body can't work without them. They give you energy, build and repair your cells to stop you getting ill and keep you healthy. These are:

Let's look at them in more detail . . .

Carbohydrates

Carbohydrates – or carbs – are broken down by the body into simple sugars, which provide us with loads of energy. Most foods contain carbs, but the biggest and best-known carbohydrates are potatoes, rice, bread and pasta.

Carbs should make up about a third of your diet. There are two types – **simple** and **complex**.

Simple carbohydrates are also called **simple sugars**. You can find these simple carbs in sweets and chocolate or in white or brown sugar. But while these will give you energy, you're better off getting your simple carbs from fruit, milk, yoghurt or breakfast cereal. That's because these foods also contain vitamins, fibre, calcium and other good stuff.

Complex carbohydrates are also called **starches**. These include pasta, bread, rice, etc. They contain vitamins and minerals and fibre – which helps your digestive system work. Again, while they will give you energy, it's better to go for wholemeal bread or brown rice because they often contain extra fibre and vitamins.

Which carbs should you eat? Well, both types are important in a healthy diet. But remember: complex carbohydrates help you to feel full up – so you'll feel more satisfied than if you just eat sugary treats with simple carbs. These simple carbs give us a burst of energy very quickly, but it doesn't last very long and soon after you'll feel very tired. But the energy from complex carbohydrates lasts much longer!

Protein

Protein is important to keep our muscles, organs and immune system strong and healthy. Some can be made in the body, but others can only come from food and drink.

Protein is digested more slowly than carbohydrates. That means you stay comfortably full up for longer after eating. Protein is also very important for mending our bodies – people who don't get enough protein in their diet may find their cuts and scratches take more time to heal.

Protein-rich foods should make up around 10–30% of your diet. There are two types – **animal proteins** and **vegetable proteins**.

Animal proteins are found in foods like fish, meat, eggs, milk, cheese and yoghurt.

Vegetable proteins are found in foods such as chickpeas, beans, lentils, tofu, seeds and nuts.

GUESS WHAT?

Without a protein called **albumin**, made in your liver, fluid can build up in your body, making some parts – such as your feet, hands, belly and legs – swell up!

Fats

Fats are a very important part of a healthy diet and give you lots of energy. They are usually rich in vitamins to make you healthier too. Fats also insulate your body to keep you warm and help your brain and nervous system to work properly. They also give our food lots of flavour and texture.

There are three types of fats:

Unsaturated fats – these are good for your heart. You find them in foods such as salmon, avocados, nuts and vegetable oils.

Saturated fats – you find these in meat, butter, cheese and also palm oil and coconut oil.

Trans fats – these are in margarine, and often in snack foods – like cakes and biscuits. But these fats aren't as good for you as unsaturated fats.

Fats are a key part of your diet and should make up between 20–35% of it. But remember, it's all about choosing a good combination of foods – you certainly wouldn't want 20% of your diet to be trans fats. If you're getting most of your fats from meat, fish and healthy oils, then you're on the right track!

Vital Vitamins

Vitamins are those nutrients that your body needs in small doses to stay healthy and keep everything working. The best way to get all the vitamins we need is through a balanced diet!

There are thirteen different vitamins, and each has a special job to do in the body. Think of them like collectables – wouldn't it be awesome to have a full set? Well, you CAN!

DIFFERENT FOODS CONTAIN DIFFERENT VITAMINS AND BY HAVING A BALANCED AND HEALTHY DIET YOU CAN MAKE SURE YOU GET THEM ALL.

Some of the vitamins that you get from food – vitamins A, D, E and K – dissolve in fat and are stored inside the body. They hang out in your body fat and in your liver, waiting for the time when your bloodstream will take them to where they're needed.

Some of the others that you get from your food – the B vitamins and vitamin C – dissolve in water so they can't be stored in your bloodstream. Your body absorbs some of the goodness, but the rest is peed out. Our bodies have to replace them so we need to eat more of the foods that contain them.

CONTEST OF THE

Vitamin A

I give your eyesight a big boost. Night vision? That's me. Colour vision? Yep, me too. And I'm a great pal to your immune system! You can find me in – **Spinach! Sweet potatoes! Carrots! Kale! Liver! Fortified milk! And more!**

The B Vitamins

We're a supergroup. The eight of us help you transform the food you eat into energy when you need it most. We also help make red blood cells, which take oxygen all over your body! You can find us in – **Fish! Chicken! Eggs! Milk! Yoghurt! Beans! Peas! Fortified cereal! And more!**

Vitamin C

The C is for Caring! I'm here to look after your gums, bones and blood vessels! If you get a cut, I'll help you heal. I also help your body absorb iron. And if you get sick, it's me – Caring C – who'll help you get better faster. You can find me in – **Tomatoes! Strawberries! Broccoli! Cabbage! Citrus fruits! Red peppers! And more!**

VITAMINS!

Vitamin D

I'm tough. You see, I help you grow strong, healthy bones and teeth. I must be the brightest vitamin too, as I'm produced when the sun lands on your skin! Of course you can find me in food too. I'm in – **Milk! Fish! Egg yolks! Fortified cereal! Liver! And more!**

Vitamin E

I'm the best at keeping your skin in great shape. I also look after your eyes, protect your cells and strengthen your immune system, so you can fight off nasty bugs. You can find me in – **Vegetable oils! Wheat! Oats! Leafy green vegetables! Egg yolks! And more!**

Vitamin K

I live in your blood and help wounds to heal by clotting! I also help bones stay healthy. You can find me in – **Broccoli! Olive oil! Leafy green vegetables! Milk! Yoghurt! And more!**

So which vitamins are best? **ALL OF THEM!** Your body needs each and every one to keep it working.

The naming of vitamins is a funny thing. For instance, the B vitamins are known as B1, B2, B3, B5, B6, B7, B9 and B12.

You may have noticed some missing numbers. The gaps are there because scientists made mistakes. Remember, a vitamin is an essential nutrient that we need to grow that can't be made inside the body – if you don't have it in your diet, you'll get sick. So most of the missing vitamins weren't really vitamins after all or were just a slight variation on a vitamin that already existed. For instance, vitamin G had its name changed to vitamin B2!

Most of the downgraded vitamins are still available as supplements to help keep the body healthy. For instance, vitamin F was the old name for omega-3 and omega-6, which are essential fatty acids.

GUESS WHAT?

Vitamin K is named after the Danish and German word Koagulation. In English, the word is spelled coagulation and is another word for blood clotting.

B1 B3 ?

B2 B5

? B6

B7 B12

B9 ?

MIGHTY MINERALS

It might seem strange that our bodies need minerals to work properly. Don't minerals come out of the ground?

Well, minerals are found inside living things too. Like vitamins, your body needs them to stay in tiptop condition. They keep your bones, heart, brain and muscles working well. They also help the chemical reactions inside your body to happen.

Let's look at some of the most important minerals at work inside your body.

Calcium
When it comes to healthy bones and teeth, calcium is number one. You get calcium from – **Milk! Cheese! Yoghurt! Beans! Tinned salmon! And more!**

Zinc
Zinc helps you fight off germs so it's great for your immune system. You get zinc from – **Beef! Pork! Milk! Cheese! Yoghurt! Nuts! Lentils! And more!**

Fibre

Fibre is a type of carbohydrate, but the body can't break it down – so it passes through our bodies and into our large intestine. It's very important in keeping our digestive system healthy and making sure all the food and waste moves through your body as it should! You can find it in a lot of plant-based foods such as beans, nuts, vegetables and wholegrains.

Iron

This stuff is vital for your red blood cells, which carry oxygen through your body. Have you ever had a nosebleed and noticed a metal taste at the back of your throat? That's iron! You'd feel weak and faint without it. You get iron from – **Meat! Tuna! Salmon! Eggs! Beans! Chickpeas! Spinach! And more!**

Potassium

Your muscles, heart and nervous system need potassium to keep working properly. You get potassium from – **Bananas! Tomatoes! More bananas! Potatoes! Oranges! Beans! And more!**

Water

You know when you come in from playing outside, and you feel hot and thirsty and you're red in the face? That's your body telling you that you're **dehydrated** – you need water to help you **rehydrate**. So get drinking – you need between six to eight glasses a day.

Without water, none of us would be here. Water is very important to life. The human body can survive for weeks without food, but it can only last a few days without water.

JOE KNOWS

At least 60% of an adult human body is made of water.

As well as tasting good, water is needed inside your body. For instance:

1. **Water keeps your blood and cells working.**
   Lots of chemicals dissolve in water. This lets your body absorb them, bringing nutrients and oxygen to your cells.

2. **Water helps your body stay at a good temperature.**
   When it's hot, any extra heat leaves the body as sweat (which is around 99% water) to help cool us down.

3. **Water keeps your joints happy.**
   The fluid in the body that greases your joints so they work smoothly is made mostly of water. Without it, you'd be quite stiff and sore.

4. **Water flushes out the waste.**
   Water helps your liver and kidneys to dissolve nasty waste products so you can pee them out. If you're drinking enough water, your pee is clear and not smelly. If you're not drinking enough, your pee will be darker and smell – and your colon will take too much water from your poo, making it hard to push out.

Balanced Diet

Now you might be feeling a little overwhelmed by all those different kinds of foods and thinking where do you even start? But remember that it's all about balance. You want to make sure you're getting enough carbohydrates, proteins, fats, vitamins and minerals in your diet. It's okay to have a sweet treat every now and then – but certainly not all the time, as your body won't get the nutrients it needs to keep you happy and healthy.

The Healthy Plate

Take a look at this plate and think about some of the foods that you could put on to it to make a balanced meal.

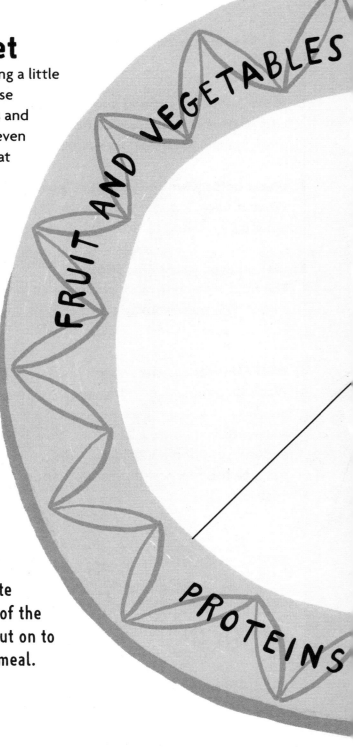

FRUIT AND VEGETABLES

PROTEINS

CARBOHYDRATES

OILS & SPREADS

DAIRY

FRUIT AND VEGETABLES – we should eat at least five portions of fruit and vegetables a day and they should make up just over a third of our diet.

CARBOHYDRATES – foods such as potatoes, wholewheat rice and pasta come into this section and should make up about a third of our diet.

PROTEINS – animal and vegetable proteins such as meat, fish, nuts and beans should make up around 10–30% of our diet.

DAIRY – dairy products such as cheese, milk and yoghurts are important for calcium and should make up around 10% of our diet.

Don't forget that foods like chocolate, crisps, cakes and biscuits are high in fat, salt and sugar – so we should only eat them in small amounts.

CHALLENGE: Eat a Rainbow

Eating a rainbow means filling your plate with fruits and vegetables of different colours. It's a good idea — not just so your plate looks cool, but because the things that give foods their colour can also give good things to you!

CAN YOU FIND A FRUIT OR VEGETABLE FOR EVERY COLOUR OF THE RAINBOW? GIVE IT A GO! HERE'S SOME IDEAS TO GET YOU STARTED.

Red foods
tomatoes, strawberries, cherries, raspberries, red peppers, watermelon

Orange foods
carrots, oranges, sweet potatoes, apricots, butternut squash

Yellow foods
bananas, sweetcorn, peaches, pineapple

Green foods
courgettes, cabbage, broccoli, green beans, apples, pears

Purple foods
red cabbage, radishes, beetroot, grapes, blackberries, purple potatoes

White foods
mushrooms, onions, leeks, potatoes

JOE'S TOP TEN FOODS

I've given you a lot of information on the great stuff our bodies take from food in order to keep fit and healthy. But talking about it is one thing – how about we start EATING?

Here are some of my favourite foods – not only because they're tasty, but because they're full of good stuff. How do they compare to your most marvellous meals?

1 Eggs
I love eggs – they're the ultimate superfood. Full of protein and healthy fats, I love them scrambled, poached or in omelettes!

2 Milk
Loads of good stuff in cow's milk. Nowadays, I actually prefer almond milk and oat milk – but it's all a matter of taste. And that taste is YUM!

3 Stir-fry vegetables
One of my go-tos for a healthy meal is veggies fried in a wok. You can ask an adult to cut them up – or get a bag of ready-prepped stir-fry vegetables from the shops. From pan to your plate in just a few minutes!

4 Chicken
Yes! Full of protein that's going to help me bounce back fast from a good workout.

5 Salmon

Also a fabulous protein source. Mmm, and high in B vitamins, potassium and other minerals . . .

6 Berries

I always have these in my fridge – strawberries, raspberries, blueberries, blackberries. Great in smoothies or on porridge in the morning or just as a tasty dessert or snack.

7 Pasta

Pasta is a great way to have a super-healthy, extra-speedy meal. Throw in some of those stir-fried veggies or some pesto and it'll taste delicious.

8 Orange marmalade

I love this stuff on toast – it's one of my favourite foods!

9 Greek yoghurt

Great for yummy puddings. Just add berries or a bit of granola – or eat it on its own! It always hits the spot.

10 Lemons and limes

I drink a lot of water and I like to add a slice of lemon or lime to give it a fruity, zesty, kick.

93

Why don't you make a list of your favourite foods here?

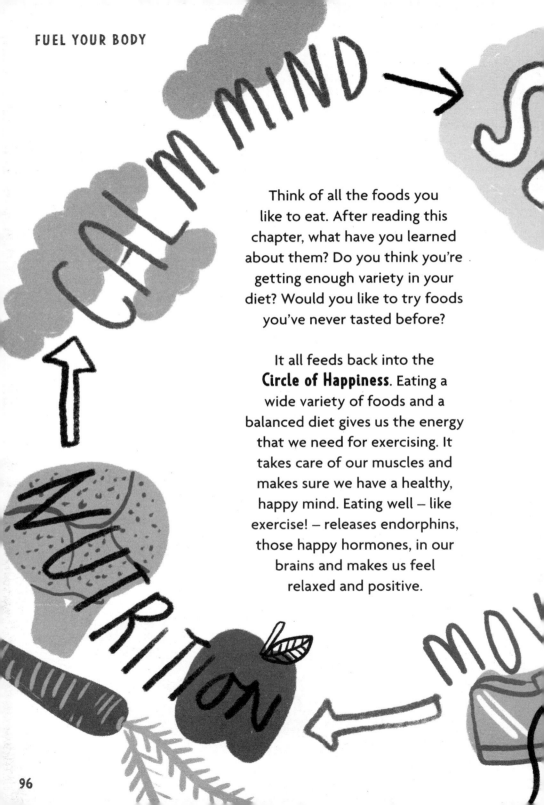

CALM MIND

S

NUTRITION

MOV

Think of all the foods you like to eat. After reading this chapter, what have you learned about them? Do you think you're getting enough variety in your diet? Would you like to try foods you've never tasted before?

It all feeds back into the **Circle of Happiness**. Eating a wide variety of foods and a balanced diet gives us the energy that we need for exercising. It takes care of our muscles and makes sure we have a healthy, happy mind. Eating well – like exercise! – releases endorphins, those happy hormones, in our brains and makes us feel relaxed and positive.

PROFESSOR JOE'S FOOD QUIZ

Test how much you can remember from chapter 2 with this quick quiz! If you get stuck, flick back to the pages before.

1 Which of these is not one of the seven essential nutrients?
a) Proteins b) Carbohydrates c) Neurons d) Fats

2 What are the two types of protein?
a) Animal and vegetable
b) Simple and complex
c) Complex and animal
d) Simple and vegetable

3 What is the name of the protein made in your liver?
a) Cells b) Cilia c) Fats d) Albumin

4 Which vitamin takes care of your eyesight?
a) Vitamin K b) Vitamin D c) Vitamin A d) Vitamin B2

5

What vitamin is produced when the sun lands on your skin?

a) Vitamin D b) Vitamin K
c) Vitamin E d) Vitamin A

6

Which word is Vitamin K named after?

a) Keratin b) Koagulation
c) Knee d) Kidneys

7

Which mineral keeps your teeth and bones strong?

a) Zinc b) Calcium c) Iron
d) Potassium

8

How much of the adult human body is water?

a) At least 10% b) At least 20%
c) At least 60% d) None

9

Which of these foods are not in Joe's rainbow foods?

a) Tomatoes b) Beetroot
c) Cheese d) Broccoli

10

Which of these is not one of Joe's top ten foods?

a) Eggs b) Berries c) Salmon
d) Lollipops

To check your answers turn to page 192.

CHAPTER 3

MOVE YOUR BODY!

Moving your body every day is really important.
All movement is good for you, but exercise that gets
your blood pumping builds up your strength and
helps you to sleep better and feel happier mentally.
So what are you waiting for?

LET'S GET MOVING!

Regular exercise is brilliant for so many reasons.
Here are just a few:

Exercise gets your heart pumping faster. The more your heart beats, the more blood gets pushed round your body. The blood delivers oxygen to your cells to keep them in tiptop condition and flushes away any bad stuff. It's like cleaning your body from the inside!

Exercise helps your joints move more easily, builds up muscle and strengthens your bones. Your heart and lungs will work more efficiently too, so you'll have extra energy to tackle each new day.

Exercise releases **endorphins** in your brain that make you feel good and reduce stress.

ZZZZz

Exercise helps you sleep more easily and you'll also be able to think more clearly, concentrate for longer and improve your memory!

There really is no downside to keeping yourself fit and active! And, as anyone who's ever played a game of tag or chase, or danced or skipped or kicked a ball about will know, the biggest upside is that it's **FUN!**

EXERCISE WISE

Now you may think that exercise is just running about or jumping, but there are lots of different types such as:

Warm Up

Cool Down

Endurance exercises (also called aerobic exercises)

Strength exercises

Balance exercises

Flexibility exercises

Now, as with the food we eat, it's important that we choose a variety of these, as each one is good for our body in different ways. But the great news is that whichever exercise you do, it improves your ability to do the others. It's magic!

WARM UP

Warming up is very important because it prepares you for the activity you're about to do. It helps get the blood flowing and allows more oxygen to reach your muscles. It also improves the communication between your nervous system and your muscles, and that means you're able to move easily.

It's important to make sure your warm-up routine has some **stretching** in it. This reduces the risk of hurting yourself or having sore muscles the next day!

BEFORE WE LEARN A BIT MORE ABOUT THE DIFFERENT WAYS TO EXERCISE, LET'S WARM UP.

CHALLENGE: Warm Up

March on the Spot

This one does what it says on the tin — you just stand up and march on the spot! Make sure you get your knees high up in the air.

Try doing this ten times.

Touch those Toes

Keep your feet wide
apart. Bend forward
and twist to touch
your right foot with
your left hand. Then
swap and touch your
left foot with your
right hand. Pick up the
pace and build up a
nice rhythm.

Try to do
this ten times
on each side.

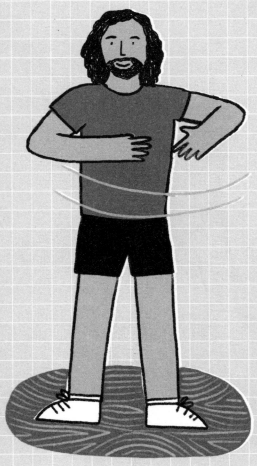

Let's Twist Again

Standing up straight, hold your arms out in front of you, bent at the elbows — like you're holding on to really wide handlebars. Then twist your upper body from side to side.

Try doing this ten times.

Work on those Circles

Standing up tall with your arms straight down by your sides, lift them up above your head and then, in a windmill motion, make big circles in the air. Make the circles go forwards, then make the circles go backwards.

Try doing this ten times.

LOVELY JOB! HOPEFULLY YOU'RE NOW FEELING WARM AND READY TO MOVE.

IMPORTANT:
DON'T FORGET TO LISTEN TO YOUR BODY! EXERCISE SHOULDN'T MAKE YOU FEEL DIZZY OR LIGHT-HEADED, AND YOU SHOULDN'T FEEL ANY PAIN OR PRESSURE IN YOUR CHEST. IF YOU DO, STOP IMMEDIATELY AND SPEAK TO AN ADULT.

GUESS WHAT?

If you're dehydrated, you'll find exercise much harder. So make sure you drink plenty of water!

ENDURANCE EXERCISES

Endurance exercises move the muscles in your arms and legs. They get your heart pumping and make you breathe harder so your body grows stronger. They're called **endurance exercises** because you repeat the same moves over and over again – like star jumps (see page 114) or swimming or running. Endurance exercises are also known as **aerobic exercises**.

These exercises generally make us fitter and help improve the function of our heart, lungs and circulation. If you do exercises like this, you'll also find that they'll make all the other movements you do each day much easier.

AEROBIC EXERCISE IS KEY TO GETTING THE HEART PUMPING, TAKING IN OXYGEN AND TO KEEPING YOUR DIGESTION HEALTHY.

JOE KNOWS!

A lot of my workouts are based around doing aerobic exercises for thirty seconds, then having thirty seconds to rest before doing the next lot. It's called **interval training** and it's really effective. In fact, tests have shown that a short burst of exercise for five or ten minutes a few times each day boosts your brainpower. You can time your thirty-second intervals using a watch, a clock, a phone or a kitchen timer.

CHALLENGE: Climb the Rope

DON'T FORGET TO KEEP YOUR KNEES NICE AND HIGH.

1. Imagine there's a long rope hanging down from the ceiling (or from a cloud if you're exercising outside).

2. Run on the spot and reach your hands up into the air.

3. Now imagine you're pulling that rope down from the ceiling, one hand at a time.

THIS IS ONE OF MY FAVOURITE ENDURANCE EXERCISES.

How many times can you do this in thirty seconds? Write down your score — then challenge yourself to beat it next time!

CHALLENGE: Star Jumps

1. Stand upright with your legs together and arms straight by your sides.

2. Bend your knees and jump. Widen your legs so you land with your feet apart.

3. At the same time, bring both hands together above your head.

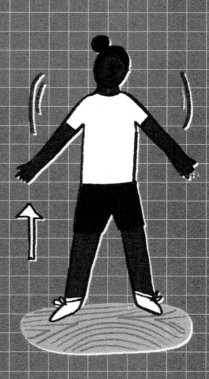

4. Jump again, only this time land with your feet together and bring your arms back down by your sides.

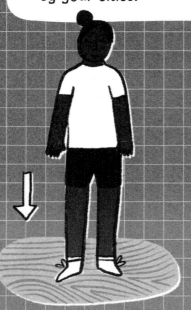

Repeat the process as many times as you can in . . .

60 SECONDS!

STRENGTH EXERCISES

These exercises help your muscles get stronger so you can exercise for longer. Every time you do push-ups or sit-ups, burpees or stair-climbing – even if you're helping to carry the shopping – you're working on your muscle strength. If you do strength exercises regularly, you'll soon notice that your muscles feel much stronger.

SOME OF MY **FAVOURITE** STRENGTH EXERCISES ARE **SQUATS, BURPEES** AND **THE PLANK.**

LET'S TRY SOME **SQUATS!**

CHALLENGE: Squats

1. Stand with your feet apart, a bit wider than your hips, and your toes slightly turned out.

2. Keeping your back straight, push out your bum and bend your legs at the knees. Keep your knees behind your toes!

3. Sit in this squatting position as if you're perched on an invisible chair. Make sure your heels and toes are flat on the floor.

4. Press down into your heels to raise yourself back to a standing position.

Try five of these to start with. Then take a break and try five more!

REMEMBER, THEY MIGHT BE TOUGH TO START OFF WITH, BUT THE MORE YOU PRACTISE THE EASIER IT WILL GET.

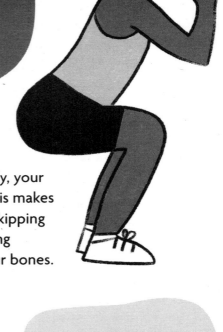

GUESS WHAT?

Squats use the biggest and strongest muscles in your body – your quadriceps, hamstrings and gluteus maximus (see page 29)

But strength exercises aren't just for your muscles. They help with your bones too! When your arms, legs or feet support the weight of your body, your muscles push against your bones. This makes them bigger and stronger. If you're skipping with a rope, dancing, running or lifting something, you're strengthening your bones.

JOE KNOWS!

If you're finding your workout a bit tough, why don't you put on your favourite music? Lots of people believe that music helps us exercise for longer and puts us in a good mood.

BALANCE EXERCISES

These strengthen the muscles in your back, your legs and your **abdomen** (the part of your body between your chest and your hips) so your body feels more stable when you move about. Balance is really important for lots of things we do – standing up, bending over to tie up our laces or riding a bike.

DOING YOGA, STANDING ON ONE LEG OR STANDING ON A WOBBLE BOARD WITHOUT FALLING OFF ARE GREAT BALANCING ACTIVITIES.

CHALLENGE: Sit to Stand

1. Sit on the floor cross-legged.

2. Now, without pushing against the floor with your hands, try to stand up just by using your legs.

CAN YOU KEEP YOUR BALANCE?

UP

DOWN

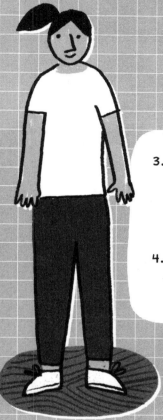

3. Keeping your feet crossed, lower your body back down into a cross-legged position.

4. Now raise yourself back into a standing position as before.

Balance is like using your muscles – the more you practise, the better it will become. So it's very important you include some balance activities in your exercise routine.

UP

JOE KNOWS!

Eyesight is really important for your balance. Try standing on one leg – did you find that pretty easy? Next, try standing on one leg and looking up at the ceiling. Was that a bit harder perhaps? Okay, now try it a third time, but with both eyes closed. Did you wobble?

Your eyes give your brain important information about where you are in the space around you. This is why it's much harder to balance when your eyes are closed!

FLEXIBILITY EXERCISES

These are all about **stretching**. They keep your body supple – which means your muscles don't get too tense – and help you move your joints properly.

CAN YOU TOUCH YOUR TOES? IF THE ANSWER IS YES, THAT MEANS YOU'RE PRETTY FLEXIBLE.

WHAT ARE YOUR FAVOURITE YOGA POSES?

Yoga is a great way to work on your flexibility. It's a form of exercise that has lots of really helpful stretches for your body and helps you to concentrate and relax.

CHALLENGE: Cat-cow Stretches

1. Start on all fours with your back flat and your eyes looking down at the floor.

2. Breathe in and drop down your tummy while slowly lifting up your head and neck. This is the cow part of the pose!

3. Breathe out, lift your tummy, move your head so you're looking at your belly button and arch your back like a cat.

Repeat steps two and three! Try this ten times.

Flexibility exercises are a great way to relax or unwind if you're feeling a little anxious or worried. This is because they help you to think about the body's connection to the mind, and encourage you to focus on something else .

IF YOU PRACTISE A LITTLE BIT EACH DAY, YOU'LL SOON FIND YOURSELF BEING ABLE TO DO THINGS THAT YOU COULDN'T DO BEFORE!

CHALLENGE: Stepping Stones

Each morning, sit on the floor and put your legs together, straight out in front of you. Now reach your arms forward and try to touch your toes.

At first you may not be able to reach that far, but day by day you should get a little closer. Once you can touch your toes don't stop there! Now you can start trying to touch your knees with your nose!

IMPORTANT: Don't push yourself too far. As with any stretch, only do it until you feel a gentle ache in your muscles and **STOP** straight away if it hurts.

COOL DOWN

After you've finished exercising, it's a good idea to take a few moments to cool down. It's very important after a workout because it allows your heart rate and body temperature to return to their normal levels in a more controlled way. You're also less likely to get any cramps or stiffness if you stretch your muscles while they're still warm.

TURN OVER FOR SOME GREAT COOL-DOWN ACTIVITIES!

Slo-mo Dance

Dance in slow motion for thirty seconds. Take a twenty-second break, then start dancing again! Why not work out a slo-mo routine with your friend?

Down and Up

Bend down and touch your toes for twenty seconds. Then slowly straighten up and stretch your arms above your head and touch the sky for twenty seconds! **Repeat.**

Heels and Toes

Walk in a wavy line on tiptoes for twenty seconds, then walk back to where you started on your heels. **Repeat.**

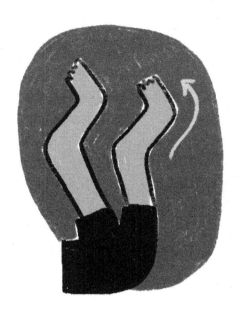

Pedal

Lie on your back with your legs and feet in the air. Then imagine you're riding an invisible bike and pedalling through the air. Start off gently and then get a little bit faster.

Str-e-e-etch

Stand with your feet shoulder-width apart. Lock your fingers with your palms facing away from you, then stretch your arms out in front of you as far as you can. **Hold for ten seconds, rest, then repeat.**

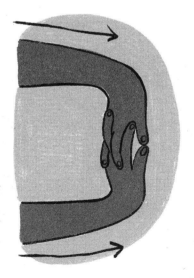

GUESS WHAT?

Stretching **after** you run is more important than stretching **before** you run. It helps clean your muscles of **lactic acid**, a chemical that your body produces when you exercise that can cause stiff muscles if it isn't removed.

DIRECT YOUR ENERGY

So now you know about the different ways to exercise. But, while exercise is fun in itself, you can also put it to good use. One really great way is to play games. Some of us love kicking a ball about the playground while others prefer swimming or gymnastics or playing chase. It's also a great way for us to spend time with friends or make new ones.

Regular exercise helps us be better, more consistent and more confident in everything we do.

THE MOST **IMPORTANT THING** IS TO ENJOY GETTING BETTER AT PHYSICAL ACTIVITY IN **YOUR OWN TIME** AND **YOUR OWN WAY.**

Any form of exercise – whether at home or at school – will see you develop your **physical skills**. Here are some of the key physical skills to think about:

POWER

REACTIONS

AGILITY

Mobility
BALANCE
SPEED

You know how reading and writing help you develop your literacy skills? Well, exercising and playing more sports and games helps you develop your **physical skills** – in other words, they help your body to move confidently through the world around you.

LET'S LOOK AT EACH OF THESE KEY WORDS IN MORE DETAIL.

POWER

What do you get if you combine **speed** and **strength**? POWER! Power is the ability to use your muscle strength quickly and with control. You use power to achieve a goal in a particular time by being fast and strong – like playing football or performing a gymnastics routine.

Are you great at catching a ball or hitting a shuttlecock with a racket? Then clearly you've got very good reactions!

Good reactions are all about how quickly you respond to something happening. Remember back on page 34, I told you about the way your brain sends electrical signals through your body to make it respond in a certain way? It's this skill that allows you to catch a ball or skip with a skipping rope or play Frisbee.

The more you practise, the faster your reactions will become, and the better you'll get at an activity!

CHALLENGE: Reaction Rate

You need a friend, or family member, and a ruler. Ask the person you choose to hold the top of the ruler, pointing down, and then put your hand underneath with your thumb and index finger slightly open, ready to catch it.

DOWN

Get your friend to drop the ruler and try to catch it as quickly as you can. You can measure how well you did by how far up the ruler your fingers are. The lower the number the better.

KEEP PRACTISING AND SEE IF YOU CAN BEAT YOUR QUICKEST REACTION TIME!

AGILITY

If you're agile, it means you have good speed, balance and physical coordination. In other words, you can run and jump and twist and slide and change direction quickly and easily. Basketball players are very agile, as they duck and dive round their opponents.

HAVE YOU EVER DONE A CONE DRILL WHEN YOU'VE HAD TO RUN BETWEEN CONES ARRANGED IN A CERTAIN WAY? THAT'S THE SORT OF EXERCISE THAT INCREASES YOUR AGILITY.

Mobility

Mobility is being able to move your whole body freely. Good muscle strength, flexible joints and plenty of endurance help our bodies to move well. It also gives us good posture and helps prevent injuries.

BALANCE

At its most basic, balance is about staying in a particular position. For example, if you're riding a bike, you don't want to wobble so much you fall off! There aren't many exercises where balance isn't required. Your ability to keep your body still and stable – especially when you change position or take one leg off the ground – is an incredibly useful skill.

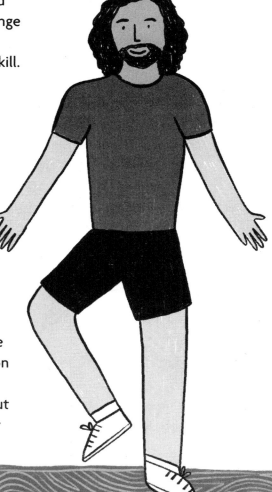

TURN BACK TO PAGE 119 TO REMIND YOURSELF OF SOME OF MY **FAVOURITE BALANCE** EXERCISES.

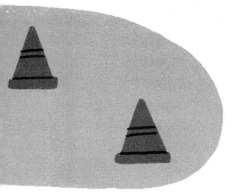

Have you got good balance? Have you ever tested it? Try standing on one leg and see if you can keep your balance. Now try it again, but this time on tiptoe. Was it harder this time or easier?

SPEED

Speed is important for most sports, but it isn't only about running really quickly. Often in sport it's about working fast enough to achieve a victory – like swimming, or hurdling or even horse riding! Our speed often improves as our muscles get stronger.

GUESS WHAT?

The fastest man on earth is the sprinter Usain Bolt. He once ran 100 metres in just 9.58 seconds!

ALL TOGETHER NOW!

I love to exercise on my own, but it's also great fun to exercise with others. I've put together a list of some of my favourite things to do with my family and friends for you to try!

PLAY TENNIS

PLAY FOOTBALL

HAVE A RUNNING RACE

PLAY A GAME OF ROUNDERS

PLAY A SKIPPING GAME

DANCE TO MUSIC

Turn over for some more fun games to play with friends and family.

CHALLENGE: Ladder Challenge

Use low-tack tape (like masking tape), or use coloured chalk, to make a ladder on a patio or flat safe surface like a driveway. Give it at least ten rungs and leave a gap large enough between each rung to step in.

PLEASE MAKE SURE YOU GET PERMISSION FROM A TRUSTED ADULT BEFORE YOU START.

With a ladder challenge, you can make your own rules.

Will you jump between every other rung? Will you hop into each space up and down the ladder on one foot?

Will you jump into the first space on one foot, then jump again with both feet outside the ladder before jumping into the third space on one foot again?

It's up to you, but the faster you go, the more you'll test your speed, balance and agility!

CHALLENGE: Hula-Hoopla

If you have hula hoops of different colours, lay them out in your nearest park or garden. If you don't have any, try drawing circles using coloured chalk on a safe surface like a driveway or patio.

PLEASE MAKE SURE YOU GET PERMISSION FROM A TRUSTED ADULT BEFORE YOU START.

Then decide who'll be the Caller. The Caller tells the other players which hoop they must jump into.

They can either choose a sequence of colours that the players have to remember, or shout out whatever order they like.

Remember that the bigger the distance there is between hoops, the bigger the challenge and the wilder the fun!

CHALLENGE: Up and At 'Em

All players choose the same starting position on the floor – lying face down, squatting, curled up in a ball, etc.

The Caller shouts an instruction, like:

RUN TO THE FAR WALL!

JUMP UP AND HOP ON YOUR LEFT LEG FIVE TIMES!

LIE DOWN FLAT!

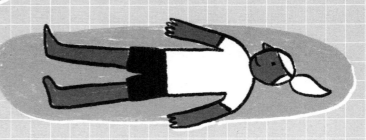

GET UP,
SPIN ROUND
TEN TIMES!

DO
FIVE BUNNY HOPS
AND THREE SNOW
ANGELS!

The players must leave their starting positions and follow the instructions as quickly as possible, however wacky or complicated they become!

THE WINNER
IS THE ONE WHO FINISHES
FIRST – OR WHO BEATS THEIR
PREVIOUS BEST TIME!

Now we've gone through a lot of the different ways your body can exercise, you can see why I spent a long time in chapter 2 talking about how you have to feed it properly. We need the right foods to give us the energy to do all this exercise, and in turn the exercise fuels our hearts and heads, keeping us alert and giving us happy feelings.

THIS ALL ADDS UP TO A **HEALTHY BODY!**

I hope this chapter has given you some ideas and inspiration for your exercise. The key to it all is finding an activity you really enjoy – whether that's **karate, contemporary dance** or **BMX riding!** That way you'll always want to do it, your **physical** skills will develop and exercise will feel easy. Plus, joining a sports team or starting a new hobby is a fantastic way to make friends!

notes

You may not find that perfect PE recipe straight away, but I bet you'll have a great time along the way. And if you keep an exercise log, you'll be able to see how much time each week you've spent exercising. This is a great way to record how much physical activity you do so you can see how you're getting along. Ideally, you should be aiming to do at least **sixty minutes** of physical activity each day. But don't worry too much — if one week you don't do as much as the week before, that's okay! **The important thing is to keep going and do as much as you can.**

Start off by filling in the **exercise log** on the next page — then copy this grid on to a piece of paper to use next time.

CHALLENGE: Exercise Log

Have you ever stopped to count how many minutes of exercise you do each day? No?

Well, you should be aiming for at least 60 minutes of physical activity a day. Don't worry, it doesn't have to be done all at once, it can be broken down into smaller chunks – so you could do something like:

- 15 minutes playing catch
- A 30-minute PE class at school
- 15 minutes of stretching when you get home

USE THIS EXERCISE LOG TO RECORD HOW MUCH PHYSICAL ACTIVITY YOU DO IN A WEEK, BOTH IN AND OUT OF SCHOOL.

TOTAL TIME DURING SCHOOL HOURS	
TOTAL TIME OUT OF SCHOOL HOURS	

	DURING SCHOOL HOURS	OUT OF SCHOOL HOURS	TOTAL
MONDAY			
TUESDAY			
WEDNESDAY			
THURSDAY			
FRIDAY			
SATURDAY			
SUNDAY			

CHAPTER 4

FOCUS YOUR BODY!

So far, we've taken a journey to see how the body works, how to eat well and how to stay active to keep our bodies in tiptop condition. But what about our minds? Our thoughts? Our feelings? You may be surprised to learn that they are also affected by your choice of food, drink and exercise — just like the rest of the body.

Put simply, a healthy body is a very important part of having a healthy mind. There are plenty of reasons for this, but a lot of it comes back to **endorphins** (see page 40) – the chemicals that your brain produces when you exercise and eat good foods.

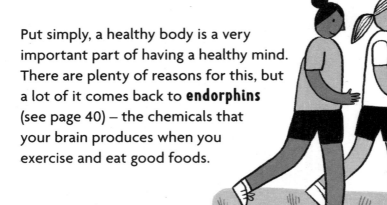

Endorphins help us to:

- Have more energy!
- Feel more confident!
- Reduce worry and stress and improve our mood!
- Sleep well at night . . . **zzzzzzzz!**

FOOD AND MOOD

Your gut is full of trillions of microbes (tiny organisms). These microbes include bacteria, fungi, viruses and all sorts of stuff. But don't be grossed out — loads of them are **friendly bacteria**, which are vital for keeping your gut and your brain **healthy and happy**. You can even get special yoghurts and yoghurt drinks full of 'live bacteria' that boost the good work that these microbes do!

Remember when we discussed your nervous system on page 34? Well, believe it or not, this is also connected to your digestive system. Your brain and stomach use your nerves to send messages to one another!

The nervous system helps you produce saliva and tells your stomach to get ready to digest food. It also sends messages to slow down your heart rate and your breathing, and this soothes your brain ready for sleep.

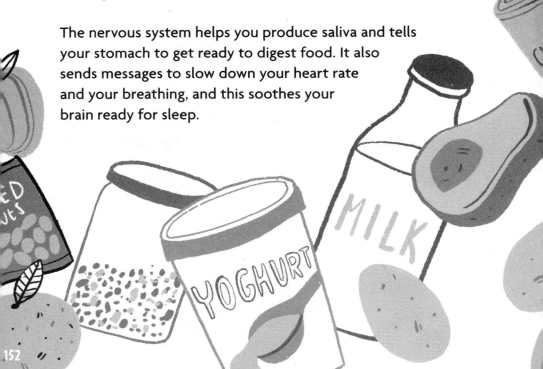

JOE KNOWS!

Ninety per cent of the **serotonin** – an important feel-good chemical that helps with sleep, memory and mood – in your brain is actually made in your digestive system!

Have you ever been worried about something and it's made you feel quite sick? Had butterflies in your tummy? Or heard the phrase 'I've got a gut feeling'? It means a kind of instinct you feel with your whole body that urges your brain to listen and act. All of these feelings are very normal and it's your brain sending messages to your digestive system about something that's making it feel anxious or worried.

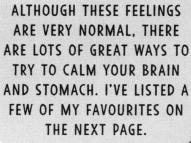

ALTHOUGH THESE FEELINGS ARE VERY NORMAL, THERE ARE LOTS OF GREAT WAYS TO TRY TO CALM YOUR BRAIN AND STOMACH. I'VE LISTED A FEW OF MY FAVOURITES ON THE NEXT PAGE.

Take some deep breaths

Breathe in through your nose, then breathe out slowly through your mouth – try five of these in a row.

Gargle

Stand next to a sink and take a sip of water from a glass. Don't swallow it though – lift your head back and gargle. Then spit it into the sink.

Get arty

Painting or doing your favourite craft is a great way to focus your mind and relax.

Sing

Belt out one of your favourite songs at top volume. You could get your friends and family to join in!

Laugh

Have you heard of **belly laughs**? They're deep and loud and hearty – the sort you make when you hear a hilarious joke! Laughing loud and proud is a great workout for your nervous system and will help boost your mood!

JOE KNOWS!

Did you ever smell yummy food and your stomach rumbled with hunger? That's because the smell made your brain think, **Ooh, lovely** and it told your stomach to stimulate your appetite. The rumbling is actually the sound of your stomach and intestine squeezing in excitement.

SO HUNGER ISN'T JUST A FEELING. IT CAN BE A NOISE AS WELL!

RUMBLE!

RUMBLE!

RUMBLE!

A HEALTHY MIND

When people talk about good mental health, it means the way that you **think and feel about yourself and the world around you**. Your mental health will affect how you cope with problems and challenges in life and the way you handle feelings of stress and anxiety.

Put simply, good mental health is when we feel **good on the inside**. Every one of us is unique. We all have different lives and will be affected by things in different ways – so there isn't a one-size-fits-all for good mental health.

It's unique to you!

And here are some of the good things that come from having a happier and healthy mind:

Feeling generally good about life.

Feeling happy about yourself – a positive self-image.

Concentrating well and focusing at school.

Feeling secure and safe at home.

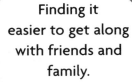

Finding it easier to get along with friends and family.

Being willing to try new things – sometimes they'll work and sometimes they won't.

Recovering more quickly if things do go wrong.

Coping with difficult feelings like anger, anxiety and sadness.

These all sound pretty good, right? You might be reading this and thinking you feel quite a few of those things already, which is great news. Or you might be thinking that none of them describe you. But that's okay too. It can help to speak to a trusted adult if anything is worrying or upsetting you. I've also included some information on page 191 of charities and networks that have further information available or have phonelines where you can talk to trained professionals who are there to help. **You don't have to go through anything alone**.

Good mental health is a tricky thing and something we all have to work towards. Remember that it's all about doing little things **one step at a time** — you'll soon find they make a big difference.

Manage The Tough Stuff

Our day-to-day lives are often very busy and we have lots of things to juggle: from relationships with our friends and family to our schoolwork. Sometimes this means we're left feeling quite overwhelmed and it's not always easy to find the right words to talk about our emotions.

Most of us can't help 'overreacting' sometimes to bad news or disappointment – we might get angry or upset. But managing our emotions is something we all have to get used to in life. It's not always easy though.

KNOW YOUR EMOTIONS!

We all know what emojis are – little pictures that sum up how we're feeling. If you're laughing at something in a message, you can send back a laughing face. If you see a picture of someone's cute pet, you can send a face with love hearts for eyes. The message is clear without needing to use words.

Here are some tips that I've always found quite helpful.

When something happens and you feel an emotion you don't like, it can seem overwhelming. But it helps if you really try to think about it.

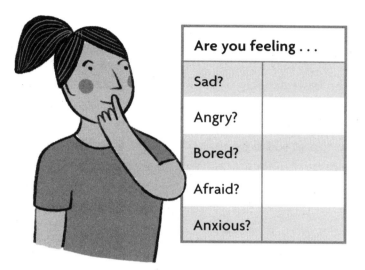

Are you feeling . . .	
Sad?	
Angry?	
Bored?	
Afraid?	
Anxious?	

Once you've named the feeling, try to label it emoji-style. For instance, if you were sad, did you feel 😕 or 😫 ? This is a really good way of working out how you're feeling and, once you're aware of your emotions, it can often help you deal with them. The fact that these emojis exist and are so common shows that everyone feels things like that.

YOU'RE NOT ALONE.

Let's Talk!

I've always found it very helpful to talk to someone when I feel upset, perhaps a family member or teacher. Sometimes just saying the words out loud will help you work through how you're feeling.

It's not always easy to start a conversation like that, and it can be a struggle to find the right words. Or you might feel that the person won't understand your situation – but remember that it's very likely they've felt the same way too at some point. My top tip for talking about your feelings is to **keep practising**. It gets easier!

And don't forget, if you spot a friend who seems a little sad or upset, why not go over and ask them how they are doing? Most people really appreciate a friendly chat when they are feeling down.

Don't Act on Impulse!

When we get angry, we sometimes do things we regret. For instance, if something makes you mad, you might want to lash out. If someone pushes you, you might want to push them back. But in both cases acting on your impulses without thinking about them can end badly.

That thing you smashed when you were angry? You really liked it, and now it's broken. You don't feel angry any more – just sad because you've made things worse for yourself.

It's hard to control impulses sometimes because feelings of anger or fear send chemicals flooding through your body so your heart pumps harder, blood brings more power to your muscles, and your blood sugar goes up to give you energy. You feel like an explosion waiting to happen!

LUCKILY, THERE ARE WAYS TO MANAGE THESE IMPULSES.

1. Deep Breaths

Big breaths are really good for calming you down – better than the shallow chest breaths we do when we're getting worked up. Counting to eight, breathe in deeply through your nose. It should feel like your chest and stomach are expanding. Then, counting to eight, breathe out through your nose. Try doing that four times.

2. Repeat! Repeat! Repeat!

When you're feeling upset, simple repetitive, rhythmic movements calm the brain. That's why rocking a baby works to soothe them. So, as well as the deep breathing, try hugging yourself and squeezing tightly every couple of seconds. Or squeeze your hands together ten times. Or touch your toes and stand up straight several times. Better yet, get on a swing and see how high you can go! The rhythmic repetition will soon have you feeling much calmer.

3. Exercise

When you feel that everything is just too much, if possible get out of the situation that's making you feel bad and exercise instead. Do some squats or jog round the field or kick a ball about. Use that energy in a good way and you'll release **endorphins** (those happy chemicals) that will help to get the angry feelings out of your system.

4. Get Some Distance

Another way to calm your mind is to go outside and stare into the distance as far as you can. When you see something that makes you feel stressed out, your eyes tend to fix on it and everything else goes blurry. This goes back to that primitive part of the brain concerned with survival – if a wolf was coming towards you, all your focus would be on it and your body would get you ready to fight or run away. So, if you look out at a horizon at nothing in particular, you will widen your gaze – and that will ease the instinct that's telling you to react.

Of course, it's easy to know what we should do, but not always easy to put it into practice. You're bound to get upset and angry at times, but try not to be too hard on yourself if you can't control your emotions. Just learn from the experience and remember these tips for a better result next time!

STRESS AND ANXIETY

Sometimes in life things happen at home or at school that make us feel unhappy. Anxious. Uneasy. **STRESSED OUT!**

You might be worried about exams. You might be afraid that your best friend has got a *new* best friend. You might be scared because you're moving house and having to start again somewhere new, or because your sports team has a big competition coming up. Whatever it is, it's filling your thoughts and sucking the fun out of life. Your head is not in a happy place. You might feel some of the following:

- a bad mood
- you lose your temper easily
- you can't sleep
- you've got no energy
- you don't want to eat (or you want to eat too much)
- headaches and stomach aches

Stress is a natural reaction! It's your body's way of handling difficult or strange situations. Not all stress is bad . . . sometimes we feel a good type of stress when we get excited, like when you ride the tallest and fastest rollercoaster! Or when it's your turn to take a penalty kick! It can get your heart pumping, help you focus and give you energy.

But stress becomes bad when you find that it's creeping into your everyday life and it's getting harder and harder to relax and bring your body back to a healthy, calm state. This kind of stress can build up and have the opposite effect to good stress: it makes you feel low and with no energy.

THERE ARE LOTS OF TIPS AND TRICKS TO HELP US MANAGE BAD STRESS AND BUILD A HAPPY MIND. HERE ARE SOME OF MY FAVOURITES:

Breathe easier

Lie on the floor on your back with a small cushion on your stomach. Count to eight and breathe in slowly through your nose. Don't breathe so that your chest rises and falls – breathe into your stomach! A good breath should expand your stomach so it swells in size. If you're getting it right, that cushion will rise up in the air as you breathe in and slowly sink back down as you breathe out.

Try doing that ten times. Swap the cushion for something you can balance on your stomach, like a ball. See if you can keep it in place by breathing slowly and steadily. The feelings of stress will start to fade as the deep breaths calm your heart rate and the repetition soothes your mind.

Play and Rest

Think about the activities that you love to do and try to do them as often as you can. The endorphins you get from doing fun things will help take your mind off the negative stuff. But make sure you leave yourself some **chilling-out time**, so you don't wear yourself out!

Exercise

Exercise is the **ultimate stress reliever!** Getting outside for some fresh air is always a good way to put you in a happier mood. Team sports can help you feel connected to other people, build friendships and boost your confidence. When you feel good about yourself, it's a great step towards a happier mind. Go on – get out there!

Write it Down

Sometimes getting your feelings down on paper, or written in a note on your phone or tablet, is a good way to 'think aloud' about whatever's bothering you. When you pin down your feelings in words, it can help you work out how you feel and cope with it a little more easily.

CHALLENGE: Dear Diary

Find one of your favourite notebooks and start keeping a diary. Try and be really honest about how you're feeling. Write down all the things (good and bad!) that have happened. See if you can keep this up for a week or longer!

Talk About It

While writing things down is a great way to work out how you really feel about something, talking things through with a friend or a trusted adult can also help you feel better. You might get some good advice and a fresh way of looking at your problems – and you won't feel like you're going through something alone.

BE MINDFUL

Mindfulness is a way of focusing your thoughts so that you stay in the moment – instead of worrying about things that happened in the past or things that might happen in the future.

Start by concentrating on your breathing – in and out – until you begin to feel calm inside. Now close your eyes and listen to the sounds you can hear around you second by second – birds singing, a car passing outside, a plane going by. Then you can think about the good things that happened in your day before turning to whatever's upsetting you. This will help you look at everything calmly.

WHY NOT TRY THE **MINDFULNESS EXERCISE** ON THE NEXT PAGE?

CHALLENGE: Mindfulness

1. Lie down in a quiet space — on your bed or on a sofa. Relax your arms and legs and close your eyes.

2. Notice how your stomach goes up and down with each deep breath. Count ten breaths.

3. Think about your day. As you breathe in, notice your stomach rising. As you breathe out, think of something that went well for you today. Repeat that with each deep breath.

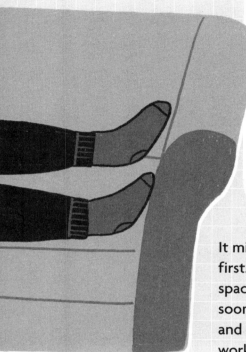

4. When you've thought of all the good things that happened, keep noticing the way your stomach rises and falls, and with every outward breath think of something you did that you're proud of. Or maybe something you'd like to happen?

5. After five minutes, wiggle your arms and legs and sit up slowly.

It might be hard to do this exercise at first. But it will get easier if you make space for mindfulness every day — and soon you may find you're feeling happier and calmer in life, and much better at working through your problems.

NOW WE GET TO ONE OF THE MOST IMPORTANT WAYS TO HAVE A HAPPY MIND AND A HEALTHY BODY (AND PERHAPS MY FAVOURITE!) . . .

SLEEEEEEEEP!

Studies have shown that young people need on average around ten hours of sleep a day.

Does that seem a lot to you? Well, remember that sleep doesn't just make sure that our body is rested. It helps us to have good mental health. As you grow up, the front area of your brain – the part that helps you set goals and controls your decision-making – is still developing.

If you don't get enough sleep, this front part of the brain is affected. Which means . . .

- Your attention span might be shorter.

- You may make bad decisions or take silly risks.

- You might struggle with your memory, and your mood may be more up and down.

- You could find it more difficult to learn in school.

- You're more likely to get ill.

- You won't be able to deal with life's challenges as well.

Routine Business!

It's not always easy to fall asleep – perhaps you end up tossing and turning and lying awake for hours. But what you need is a **good bedtime routine**. This will help train your body to expect sleep to start at a certain hour of the evening. It's also important to make sure your bedroom is a place to rest and a space to sleep – rather than busy with all your toys and schoolwork. Also make sure that it isn't too hot or too cold, as this will really affect your sleep.

JOE KNOWS!
Did you know that around 12% of people dream in black and white? Are you one of those people?

IT'S CLEAR TO SEE THAT SLEEP IS YOUR MIND'S BEST FRIEND. SLEEP RECHARGES BOTH BRAIN AND BODY AND BOOSTS YOUR IMMUNE SYSTEM. SO HOW CAN YOU MAKE SURE YOU GET MORE OF IT?

Turn over for plenty more tips on starting a good bedtime routine.

The key steps are:

• Don't eat too much before bedtime – if you're feeling full up, you won't be able to lie down comfortably.

• Try to get ready for bed at the same time each night.

• After cleaning your teeth and washing your face, try reading a book for a short time, or get someone to read to you while you close your eyes.

• Or you could listen to gentle music for a bit instead!

• Finally, turn out the lights – a nightlight is fine if you need it – and snuggle down in the darkness.

• If something is bothering you, late at night is the worst time to think about it. There's an old saying that things will always look better in the morning – and it's usually true!

• You may find that a mindfulness exercise (see page 172) helps you get off to sleep quickly.

CHALLENGE: Bedtime Boost

Start going to bed thirty minutes earlier than normal so you get more sleep.

You should start to feel happier, calmer and be able to concentrate better at school.

Even if you don't manage to fall asleep straight away, being in bed, without any distractions, will help your brain and body unwind.

SCREENS AND SLEEP DON'T MIX!

When you're lying in the dark, a special hormone called **melatonin** is released. Melatonin gives your body the signal to fall asleep. Unfortunately, the **blue light** from screens stops melatonin from forming and so delays sleepiness.

Experts reckon that you should turn off your phone or tablet at **least an hour** before you go to bed.

- To resist the temptation to check your phone, why not leave it in a different room when you go to sleep?

- Or if you use it as your alarm, put it on the other side of the room so it's not near your bed.

- Challenge yourself to make sure that something on a screen isn't the first thing you look at when you wake up.

- You could keep your favourite book or comic by your bed so you read that when you wake up!

Social Media

One of the reasons that checking our devices is so addictive is because we want to see what our friends are doing. Are they staying up late? There may be time for one last little chat – right? Maybe a few little chats . . . and before you know it, it's really late!

Unfortunately, regular late-night chats can seriously affect how well you sleep. And that can leave you too tired to work and play properly with your friends the next day!

ANOTHER WAY WE KEEP UP WITH FRIENDS – AND CELEBRITIES TOO! – IS BY FOLLOWING THEM ON SOCIAL MEDIA. THE BUZZ OF GETTING THE LATEST INFORMATION CAN BECOME A REAL HABIT.

We may feel left out if we don't know as much as our friends – or we might want to impress them by learning more than they do. Either way, if social media ever makes you feel anxious, try talking to a trusted adult about your reasons for using it.

Sleep, movement, nutrition and a calm mind.
These are all things that will keep your brain
happy and your body healthy! I've given you lots
of tips and tricks to help, so be sure to give them
a go and keep practising until you find what
works best for you!

ON THE NEXT PAGE
YOU'LL FIND A
HAPPY MIND CHART
SO YOU CAN WRITE DOWN
ALL THE EXERCISES YOU'VE
TRIED, AND WHICH ONES
MADE YOU FEEL CALMER
AND HAPPIER.

HAPPY MIND CHART

WHAT EXERCISE I DID

MONDAY	
TUESDAY	
WEDNESDAY	
THURSDAY	
FRIDAY	
SATURDAY	
SUNDAY	

HOW DID I FEEL BEFORE?	HOW DID I FEEL AFTERWARDS?

Phew! That's it, guys — we've reached the end of our journey looking at all the fantastic and wonderful things that we can do to take care of our bodies and our minds.

We now know how our body works — from the way our heart beats when we exercise, to the neurons zipping around sending messages from our brain to our body and back again. We've looked at the way our body digests food, taking all the nutrients and removing anything unwanted as waste.

Talking of nutrients . . . we looked at the key things we need to be eating and drinking to keep us fit and healthy, including those super vitamins and mighty minerals and don't forget to look out for different coloured fruits and veggies and add them into your diet.

You've got plenty of exercises to get you up and moving about, from personal challenges to games to be played with friends and family. And remember, the more you practise the easier it'll all become.

We talked about the importance of a healthy mind and getting enough sleep to make sure you are full of energy and can be your very best self every day. I hope you use lots of my tips and tricks in this chapter and start putting them to the test in your daily life.

We started with this and we have to finish with it:

...THE CIRCLE OF HAPPINESS.

CALM MIND → SLEEP
NUTRITION
MOVEMENT

You can't have a healthy body without eating good food, you won't want to eat well if you are feeling down, and exercise is one of the best ways to improve your mental health. Everything is connected.

I've had such a great time writing this book and I hope you've enjoyed reading it. And remember it's the little things that really count – just one small change every day will add up to a big difference!

Love Joe x

Acknowledgements

Putting together a book like this is always a big team effort, so I'd like to thank everyone who has made this possible.

A huge thank you to Steve Cole for working alongside me to create such an important book, and to Kate Sutton for bringing the book alive with her fabulous illustrations.

I'd like to thank the team at HarperCollins Children's Books for all their help and guidance along this journey. To Cally Poplak, Juliet Matthews, Val Braithwaite, Holly Tonks, Claire Jones, Jasmeet Fyfe, Dan Downham, Juliette Clarke, Geraldine Stroud, Elisa Offord, Sarah Lough, Sam White, Louise Ang and Alexandra Officer.

And special thanks to Alex James for taking the fabulous photos for the cover and John Di Mambro casting his expert eye over the facts.

Thank you to Bev James, my literary agent, for helping me believe in myself and building my confidence over the years. Creating children's books is a whole new world so thank you for helping make this book come to life.

Thank you to my loving wife, Rosie, for all your support in raising our children together. I learn so much from you. You, Indie, Marley and Leni bring me so much joy every day.

And finally, a huge thank you to you – the readers – for picking up my book. I hope it brings you all a fitter, healthier and happier life!

Further Information

If you're interested in knowing more about some of the topics I've discussed in this book there are lots of wonderful organisations that can tell you more:

NHS® Live Well – www.nhs.uk/live-well
A great place for advice on eating well, exercising and achieving a healthy body and mind.

NHS® Eatwell Guide – www.nhs.uk/live-well/eat-well/food-guidelines-and-food-labels/the-eatwell-guide/
A guide to what we should be eating to ensure a healthy, balanced diet.

Childline® – www.childline.org.uk or 0800 1111
A free and confidential service for under 19s in the UK where you can talk to professionals about anything that is worrying you. You can reach them at any time through their website or on the phone.

Mind® – www.mind.org.uk
A mental health charity that has lots of great advice and support for many different kinds of mental health struggles.

Young Minds – www.youngminds.org.uk
A charity with resources for both parents and children on discussing and handling mental health issues.

The Sleep Charity – www.thesleepcharity.org.uk
A charity that is focused on helping children (and adults) get a better night's sleep. They have lots of advice, education and support available on their website.

And for plenty more fun exercises and activities to keep you moving, you can check out my PE with Joe videos on my **YouTube® channel: @TheBodyCoachTV**

ABOUT

Joe Wicks

Known to millions of fans as 'The Body Coach', Joe Wicks is the bestselling author of ten cookbooks and the founder of Lean in 15. His chart-topping first book is the second highest-selling cookbook of all time. Joe's passion for fitness was sparked at a young age, and he trained as a PE teacher after graduating from his degree in Sports Science at St Mary's University in Twickenham. Joe helped to keep spirits high by becoming the 'Nation's PE Teacher' during the 2020 lockdown. Every weekday, Joe delivered remote PE sessions to children and adults alike – cementing his position as a national treasure. Through his daily live workouts, Joe has raised over £550,000 for the NHS as well as breaking a Guinness World Record after one of his PE classes was watched live by 955,000 people on YouTube. Joe Wicks was awarded an MBE in October 2020 for his work during the pandemic.

Steve Cole

A bestselling children's author with sales of over 3 million copies. His 200+ books cover many styles and genres including young series fiction (*Astrosaurs*, *Adventure Duck*); middle-grade fiction (*Z. Rex*, *Magic Ink*); Young Adult fiction (*Young Bond*, *Doctor Who*), cli-fi (*Tin Boy*, *Drowning in my Bedroom*) picture books (*Go to Sleep or I Let Loose the Leopard*) and non-fiction (*The Cosmic Diary of our Incredible Universe* with astronaut Tim Peake). He lives in Buckinghamshire and to keep fit and healthy he walks his dog and teaches salsa dancing.

Kate Sutton

Kate has been working as a freelance illustrator for the last 15 years since graduating from Leeds Metropolitan University where she studied Graphic Design. Her work includes regular editorial pieces for *The Sunday Times Magazine* and *Lonely Planet* magazine, T-shirt/textile designs and many book projects.

Here are the answers to my quizzes!

Professor Joe's Body Quiz
1)d, 2)a, 3)b, 4)c, 5)b, 6)a, 7)c, 8)a, 9)b, 10)d

Professor Joe's Food Quiz
1)c, 2)a, 3)d, 4)c, 5)a, 6)b, 7)b, 8)c, 9)c, 10)d